the PHILADELPHIA BRAND Cream Cheese

Cookbook

Published by Kraft, Inc.

Recipes and Editorial:
>   The Kraft Kitchens, Consumer Affairs
>   Department

Design, Photography, Art and Production Supervision:
>   Creative Services, Kraft, Inc.

Printed in the U.S.A.
Twelfth Printing: August, 1987

TABLE OF CONTENTS

Appealing Appetizers

Dips, spreads and more for casual or formal entertaining . . . page 13

Super Snacks and Sandwiches

Tasty tidbits and imaginative sandwiches for any day of the week . . . page 29

Special Salads and Dressings

Fruit, vegetable and gelatin salads and salad dressings for any season . . . page 41

Superb Soups and Sauces

Savory soups and versatile sauces sure to please . . . page 57

Savory Side Dishes

Vegetable, pasta and rice combinations for main course accompaniments . . . page 71

Meal Pleasing Main Dishes

Tempting casseroles and main dishes for all occasions . . . . . . page 79

Best of Breads

Delicious coffeecakes and quick breads for family and friends . . . page 93

Elegant Cheesecakes

A collection of baked and refrigerated cheesecakes for all dessert lovers . . . . . . page 107

Pies That Please

Spicy fruit pies, smooth cream pies and other pie perfections . . . page 129

Cookie Favorites

Brownies, bar cookies, drop cookies and more to keep the cookie jar filled . . . . page 141

Grand Finale

Special cakes, souffles, crepes and other sweets destined for rave reviews . . . . page 151

Table For Two

''Two-serving'' recipe ideas — from appetizers to desserts . . . . . page 169

Substitutions/Equivalents . . . . **page 182**
Index . . . . **page 185**

Introduction

Hollywood Cheesecake . . . "Philly" Fudge . . . Paradise Pumpkin Pie . . . Clam Appetizer Dip . . . Crullers . . . Savory Scrambled Eggs . . . Hot Crabmeat Appetizer . . . these are just a few of the many Philadelphia Brand cream cheese recipes featured in this anniversary collection of "good food ideas." An American original, cream cheese was developed over one hundred years ago and has since gained international fame and popularity. Today Philadelphia Brand cream cheese is an established favorite in many countries around the world.

For a bit of history — over a century ago, the first commercial cream cheese was produced by an enterprising farmer in upstate New York. The new product soon became so popular in the local area that in 1880 another cheesemaker contracted to distribute the special cheese under the trademark "Philadelphia Brand." At that time Philadelphia, already a city of great stature, was reknown for superb foods, especially dairy products.

"Philly" cream cheese became a Kraft cheese in 1928 through an opportune merger of Kraft and the Phenix Cheese Company . . . the sole producer of cream cheese. Through the years increased production, expanded use of refrigeration, improved packaging and innovative manufacturing methods have ensured the constant availability of this fresh, delicate cream cheese. Though it began modestly as a local product, Philadelphia Brand cream cheese was destined to become an American institution.

Originally, "Philly" cream cheese was used primarily as a flavorful spread for bread, toast and crackers and was also paired with preserves as a sandwich filling. Early ads touted its nutritional value stating, "For the promotion of growth, good bones, strong teeth, the child's diet must supply ample vitamin A and calcium. Philadelphia cream cheese is an excellent source of both elements."

It was not until the mid 1920s that cream cheese was used as a recipe ingredient. At that time, Kraft employed its first home economist to answer inquiries and to develop recipes for the steadily growing line of products. Cooking with cream cheese was a concept that immediately captured the attention and imagination of American homemakers. With its mild, fresh flavor, smooth texture and creamy consistency, "Philly" cream cheese was readily recognized as a versatile recipe ingredient. It blended quickly and easily with other ingredients and its mild flavor was compatible with almost any food.

One of the first recipes developed was "Kraft Philadelphia Cream Cake" which was later retitled Supreme Cheesecake. It appeared in a 1928 Kraft recipe booklet. This was quickly followed by a wide assortment of canapés, finger sandwiches, fancy fruit salads and appetizers especially designed for ladies luncheons, teas and receptions that were de rigueur in the late twenties and throughout the thirties. The now famous Frosted Sandwich Loaf made its debut at that time. Layered with colorful fillings, frosted with cream cheese and imaginatively garnished, the loaf resembled an attractive party cake.

The late 1940s and early '50s ushered in an era of cocktail parties and more casual entertaining at home. Savory cream cheese dips and spreads gained widespread popularity because they required little preparation and were easy to serve . . . not to mention, delicious! One recipe in particular gained instant fame. When Clam Appetizer Dip was first featured on the Kraft Music Hall television show, within 24 hours New York City was sold out of canned clams.

"Philly" fudges and frostings also were introduced in the 1950s. The extra creamy, no-cook fudge could be mixed in minutes and was a welcome relief from tedious candy making which required precision timing and temperatures. The unique flavor of "Philly" frostings added new appeal to traditional cakes.

In recent years the keen interest in international foods and gourmet cooking has further expanded the recipe potential of cream cheese. Mock Paté, Asparagus Delmonico, Zucchini Bisque, Poppy Seed Bread, Praline Cheesecake, German Chocolate Pie and Bavarian Apple Torte are a few of the epicurean specialities in the following chapters. Cheesecakes, which have become a favorite American dessert, are almost synonymous with Philadelphia Brand cream cheese. As witnessed by the selections in this anniversary collection, the simple cheesecake has grown more glamorous through the years. Today's versions may be marbled with chocolate, topped with meringues, garnished with kiwi fruit, flavored with peanut butter, or even made with carrots and raisins.

What began as a novel idea . . . cooking with cream cheese . . . has become an American tradition that is gaining acceptance abroad. Inspired by the "Philly" classics, imaginative cooks everywhere are constantly creating new uses for cream cheese.

Spreading cream cheese on bread, toast, crackers or bagels is still one of the most popular uses, but today it is easier . . . thanks to soft Philadelphia Brand cream cheese. Consumer needs and expectations play a key role in the development of new products. Our customers were telling us that they loved cream cheese as a spread but would like the convenience of a more spreadable product . . . so, Kraft food scientists went to work. The result was soft "Philly" cream cheese.

This new product is made with the same ingredients as traditional cream cheese and is nutritionally equivalent. The consistency, however, is significantly different. Soft "Philly" cream cheese is completely spreadable, right from the refrigerator. Although it was specifically developed as a spreading cheese, it is certainly suitable for recipes requiring spreadability and blending with chilled ingredients such as dips, spreads, frostings, cold sauces and fillings. In recipes designating regular cream cheese, soft cream cheese should not be substituted because a softer consistency may result.

The quick and easy attributes of soft cream cheese are especially welcome for instant appetizers and snacks when guests appear unexpectedly or hungry children rush home from school. Ham 'n Pickle Rollups, Creamy Deviled Eggs, "Philly" Club Sandwiches, Fruit 'n Cheese Spread and Pita Bread Sandwiches are just a few of the convenient recipes in this anniversary collection that you will want to try for family and friends.

Other recipes that have been developed for the special features of soft cream cheese are . . . Creamy Fruit Slaw, a festive combination of cabbage, apples, nuts and pineapple . . . Molded Salmon Salad, a main dish treat for luncheons and suppers . . . Honey Date Sauce, delicious on pound cake . . . Rocky Road Cheesecake, a chocolate cheesecake with marshmallows and nuts. These and many other favorites have been developed in the Kraft Kitchens especially for soft Philadelphia Brand cream cheese.

We hope you enjoy this varied collection of "good food ideas" developed through the years by the Kraft Kitchens expressly for "Philly" cream cheese. There are quick and easy recipes that can be prepared with a minimum of effort and more elegant ideas for parties and entertaining.

The Kraft Kitchens

Appetizer Paté Cheesecake — page 14
Zucchini Chive Dip — page 27
Impromptu Appetizer — page 14

Appetizer Paté Cheesecake

1 cup crushed plain croutons
3 tablespoons Parkay
  margarine, melted
    *   *   *
1 envelope unflavored gelatin
½ cup cold water
2 8-oz. pkgs. Philadelphia
  Brand cream cheese

1 8-oz. pkg. liver sausage
¼ cup Kraft mayonnaise
3 tablespoons chopped
  pimiento
2 tablespoons grated onion
1 tablespoon Kraft prepared
  mustard
½ teaspoon lemon juice

Combine croutons and margarine; press onto bottom of 9-inch springform pan. Bake at 350°, 10 minutes. Cool.

Soften gelatin in cold water; stir over low heat until dissolved. Combine softened cream cheese and liver sausage, mixing on electric mixer until well blended. Gradually add gelatin mixture, mixing until blended. Add remaining ingredients; mix well. Pour mixture over crust; chill until firm. Remove rim of pan; garnish with chopped green onion and pimiento, if desired.

Impromptu Appetizer

Be ready for unexpected guests, keep the ingredients on hand to prepare this attractive appetizer spread in a jiffy.

¼ cup cocktail sauce
1 8-oz. pkg. Philadelphia
  Brand cream cheese

Canned shrimp

Pour cocktail sauce over cream cheese; top with shrimp. Serve with crackers or party breads.

Variations: Substitute any of the following for cocktail sauce and shrimp:
- ¼ cup Kraft horseradish sauce mixed with 1 teaspoon Kraft prepared mustard and finely chopped ham
- 2¼-oz. can deviled ham and sweet pickle relish
- Crisply cooked crumbled bacon and green onion slices

"Philly" Cheese Bell

A decorative do-ahead! — serve this molded party spread with a festive array of party breads and assorted crackers. For the holidays, embellish the "bell" with red and green garnishes.

1 8-oz. pkg. Philadelphia
   Brand cream cheese
1 8-oz. container Cracker
   Barrel sharp cheddar
   flavor cold pack
   cheese food
2 teaspoons chopped
   pimiento

2 teaspoons chopped green
   pepper
2 teaspoons chopped onion
1 teaspoon Worcestershire
   sauce
½ teaspoon lemon juice

Combine softened cream cheese and cheese food, mixing until well blended. Add remaining ingredients; mix well. Mold into bell shapes using cold pack container lined with plastic wrap. Chill until firm; unmold. Garnish with chopped parsley and pimiento strips, if desired. Serve with assorted crackers.

2 bells

Variation: Prepare mixture as directed. Chill several hours or overnight. Shape into ball; roll in chopped nuts.

Mock Paté

1 8-oz. pkg. Philadelphia
   Brand cream cheese
1 8-oz. pkg. liver sausage
1 tablespoon chopped onion

1 teaspoon lemon juice
1 teaspoon Worcestershire
   sauce
   Dash of salt and pepper

Combine softened cream cheese and liver sausage, mixing until well blended. Add remaining ingredients; mix well. Chill. Serve with party rye or pumpernickel bread or assorted crackers.

2 cups

Skyline Appetizer

Serve this flavorful spread with wedges of pita bread or sesame crackers.

1 8-oz. pkg. Philadelphia Brand cream cheese
1 cup dairy sour cream
⅛ teaspoon garlic salt
⅛ teaspoon onion salt
Dash of hot pepper sauce
Rye Lace

Combine softened cream cheese, sour cream and seasonings, mixing until well blended. Chill. Garnish with shredded carrot, green onion slices or sieved egg yolk, if desired. Serve with:

Rye Lace

Party rye bread, thinly sliced
Parkay margarine, melted

Place bread on ungreased cookie sheet; brush with margarine. Bake at 325°, 10 minutes or until lightly browned. Cool. Store in airtight container.

Sausage Rolls Canadien

1 8-oz. pkg. Philadelphia Brand cream cheese
1 cup Parkay margarine
2 cups flour
2 12-oz. pkgs. smoked sausage links
Kraft prepared mustard
Poppy or toasted sesame seeds

Combine softened cream cheese and margarine, mixing until well blended. Add flour; mix well. Shape into ball; chill. Cut sausage links in half crosswise. Simmer in water 2 minutes; drain. Cool. Divide dough in half. On lightly floured surface, roll out each half to 12-inch square. Cut each square into sixteen 3 × 3-inch pieces. Spread each piece with mustard to within 1/2-inch of edge. Roll around sausage half; seal ends. Dip each roll in seeds. Place seam-side down on ungreased cookie sheet. Bake at 375°, 20 to 25 minutes or until lightly browned.

32 appetizers

Nautical Appetizers

1   8-oz. pkg. Philadelphia Brand cream cheese
1   tablespoon lemon juice
2   tablespoons chopped onion
1½   teaspoons chopped sweet pickle
1   teaspoon salt
¼   teaspoon Kraft prepared mustard
1   cup chopped cooked shrimp
    Pastry for 2-crust 9-inch pie
    Oil

Combine softened cream cheese and lemon juice, mixing until well blended. Add onion, pickle, salt and mustard; mix well. Stir in shrimp. On lightly floured surface, roll out pastry to 1/8-inch thickness; make circles with 3-inch round cutter. Place two level teaspoonfuls shrimp mixture in center of each circle. Moisten edges with cold water. Fold in half; seal edges. Fry in deep hot oil, 375°, 2 to 3 minutes or until golden brown.

Approximately 3 dozen

Variation: Substitute 6½-oz. can tuna, drained, flaked, for shrimp. Omit salt.

Hot Crabmeat Appetizer

A Kraft classic — this unique dip can be prepared in advance and baked just before guests arrive.

1   8-oz. pkg. Philadelphia Brand cream cheese
1½   cups (7½-oz. can) flaked drained crabmeat
2   tablespoons finely chopped onion
2   tablespoons milk
½   teaspoon Kraft cream style horseradish
¼   teaspoon salt
    Dash of pepper
⅓   cup sliced almonds, toasted

Combine all ingredients except nuts, mixing until well blended. Spoon mixture into 9-inch pie plate; sprinkle with nuts. Bake at 375°, 15 minutes. Serve with crackers.

"Philly" Guacamole Dip

Cream cheese gives this traditionally Mexican dip its unique flavor.

1 **8-oz. pkg. Philadelphia Brand cream cheese**	1 **tablespoon lemon juice**
2 **medium avocados, peeled, mashed**	½ **teaspoon salt**
¼ **cup finely chopped onion**	¼ **teaspoon garlic salt**
	¼ **teaspoon hot pepper sauce**
	1 **cup chopped tomato**

Combine softened cream cheese, avocado, onion, lemon juice and seasonings, mixing until well blended. Add tomato; mix lightly. Serve with corn chips or crisply fried tortillas.

4 cups

Blue Cheese Flan

This flan is a sophisticated blend of cream cheese, sour cream and blue cheese baked on a cracker crust.

¾ **cup crushed buttery crackers**	2 **4-oz. pkgs. Kraft blue cheese crumbles**
2 **tablespoons Parkay margarine, melted**	1⅔ **cups dairy sour cream**
* * *	3 **eggs**
2 **8-oz. pkgs. Philadelphia Brand cream cheese**	⅛ **teaspoon pepper**

Combine crumbs and margarine; press onto bottom of 9-inch springform pan. Bake at 350°, 10 minutes.

Combine softened cream cheese and blue cheese, mixing on electric mixer until well blended. Add 2/3 cup sour cream, eggs and pepper; mix well. Pour mixture over crust. Bake at 300°, 45 minutes. Stir remaining sour cream; carefully spread over cheesecake. Continue baking 10 minutes. Loosen cake from rim of pan. Cool; remove rim. Chill. Serve with fresh fruit and French bread.

Tropical Cheese Ball

1 8-oz. pkg. Philadelphia
  Brand cream cheese
1 8¼-oz. can crushed
  pineapple, drained
2 cups (8 ozs.) shredded
  Kraft sharp cheddar
  cheese

½ cup chopped pecans
¼ cup chopped dried apricots
1 teaspoon chopped
  crystallized ginger

Combine softened cream cheese and pineapple, mixing until well blended. Add remaining ingredients; mix well. Chill. Shape into ball; slightly flatten top. Garnish with coconut, if desired. Serve with assorted crackers.

Cucumber Cheese Spread

1 8-oz. pkg. Philadelphia
  Brand cream cheese
½ cup drained shredded
  cucumber

¼ cup finely chopped onion
1 tablespoon chopped parsley
¼ teaspoon salt
  Dash of pepper

Combine softened cream cheese and remaining ingredients, mixing until well blended. Serve with crackers.

1-1/2 cups

Hot Beef Dip

¼ cup chopped onion
1 tablespoon Parkay
  margarine
1 8-oz. pkg. Philadelphia
  Brand cream cheese,
  cubed
1 cup milk

1 4-oz. can mushrooms,
  drained
1 2½-oz. pkg. smoked sliced
  beef, chopped
¼ cup (1 oz.) Kraft grated
  parmesan cheese
2 tablespoons chopped
  parsley

Sauté onion in margarine. Add cream cheese and milk; stir over low heat until cream cheese is melted. Stir in remaining ingredients; heat thoroughly. Serve hot with chips.

2-1/2 cups

19

Curried Chicken Puffs

Show off your culinary skills for that special occasion with these miniature cream puffs stuffed with a savory chicken filling.

1 8-oz. pkg. Philadelphia Brand cream cheese
1 tablespoon milk
¼ teaspoon salt
Dash of curry powder
Dash of pepper
1½ cups chopped cooked chicken
⅓ cup slivered almonds, toasted
2 tablespoons finely chopped onion
Miniature Cream Puffs

Combine softened cream cheese, milk and seasonings, mixing until well blended. Add chicken, nuts and onion; mix lightly. Cut tops from Miniature Cream Puffs; fill with chicken mixture. Replace tops. Bake at 375°, 5 minutes or until warm.

Miniature Cream Puffs

½ cup water
¼ cup Parkay margarine
½ cup flour
Dash of salt
2 eggs

Bring water and margarine to boil. Add flour and salt; stir vigorously over low heat until mixture forms a ball. Remove from heat; cool 5 minutes. Add eggs, one at a time, beating well after each addition. Drop teaspoonfuls of batter onto ungreased cookie sheet. Bake at 400°, 30 minutes. Remove immediately from cookie sheet.

3 dozen

Clam Appetizer Dip

This dip first appeared on the Kraft Music Hall television show during the 1950 s. Within 24 hours, New York City was sold out of canned clams. Today, Clam Appetizer Dip is still a favorite.

1 8-oz. can minced clams
1 garlic clove, cut in half
1 8-oz. pkg. Philadelphia
  Brand cream cheese
2 teaspoons lemon juice

1½ teaspoons Worcestershire
  sauce
½ teaspoon salt
  Dash of pepper

Drain clams, reserving 1/4 cup liquid. Rub mixing bowl with garlic. Combine clams, clam liquid, softened cream cheese and remaining ingredients, mixing until well blended. Chill. Serve with chips or crackers.

1-2/3 cups

Seafood Appetizer Cheesecake

1 cup crushed buttery
  crackers
3 tablespoons Parkay
  margarine, melted
  *   *   *
2 8-oz. pkgs. Philadelphia
  Brand cream cheese

3 eggs
¾ cup dairy sour cream
1 7¾-oz. can salmon,
  drained, flaked
1 teaspoon lemon juice
½ teaspoon onion powder
⅛ teaspoon pepper

Combine crumbs and margarine; press onto bottom of 9-inch springform pan. Bake at 350°, 10 minutes.

Combine softened cream cheese, eggs and 1/4 cup sour cream, mixing on electric mixer until well blended. Add remaining ingredients; mix well. Pour mixture over crust. Bake at 325°, 45 minutes. Loosen cake from rim of pan. Cool; remove rim. Spread with remaining sour cream.

Variation: Substitute 6½-oz. can tuna, drained, flaked, for salmon.

Party Egg Sandwich Loaves

1 8-oz. container soft
   Philadelphia Brand
   cream cheese
1 tablespoon Kraft
   mayonnaise
1 tablespoon chopped parsley

1 medium carrot, shredded
1 hard-cooked egg
6 whole-wheat bread slices,
   crusts trimmed
3 white bread slices, crusts
   trimmed

Combine cream cheese and mayonnaise, mixing until well blended. Divide cream cheese mixture into thirds. Add parsley to one third, carrot to second third and chopped egg white to last third. For each loaf, spread one whole-wheat bread slice with 2 tablespoons parsley mixture, one white bread slice with 2 tablespoons carrot mixture and second whole-wheat bread slice with 2 tablespoons egg white mixture. Stack layers; garnish with sieved egg yolk. Cut each loaf lengthwise into thirds.

9 appetizers

Fruit 'n Cheese Spread

For your next party, fill celery or apricot halves with this tangy blue cheese spread.

1 8-oz. container soft
   Philadelphia Brand
   cream cheese
1 8¼-oz. can crushed
   pineapple, undrained

1 4-oz. pkg. Kraft blue
   cheese crumbles
¼ cup chopped nuts

Combine ingredients, mixing until well blended. Chill. Serve with sesame crackers.

2-2/3 cups

Party Egg Sandwich Loaves

Creamy Cheddar Spread

1 8-oz. container soft
   Philadelphia Brand
   cream cheese

1 8-oz. container Cracker
   Barrel sharp cheddar
   flavor cold pack cheese
   food

Combine ingredients, mixing until well blended. Serve with assorted crackers.

2 cups

Variations: Add one of the following to cheese mixture:
- 6 crisply cooked crumbled bacon slices, 1 tablespoon finely chopped onion and 1/4 teaspoon hot pepper sauce
- 2 tablespoons each finely chopped pimiento, green pepper and onion; 1/2 teaspoon lemon juice; and dash of ground red pepper
- 4-oz. can chopped green chili peppers, drained and 1 tablespoon finely chopped onion

Cheese Stuffed Celery

A favorite filling that blends quickly and easily with soft cream cheese.

1 8-oz. container soft
   Philadelphia Brand
   cream cheese
2 tablespoons Kraft blue
   cheese crumbles

Celery, cut into 3-inch
   pieces
Finely chopped nuts

Combine cream cheese and blue cheese, mixing until well blended. Fill celery with cheese mixture; sprinkle with nuts.

Variation: Omit blue cheese. Stir in 1/2 cup (2 ozs.) Kraft shredded sharp cheddar cheese, 1/4 teaspoon onion salt and dash of pepper. Fill celery; sprinkle with chopped nuts, parsley, olives or chives.

Versatile Dip

A great basic dip which lends itself to many variations — exercise your creativity.

1 8-oz. container soft Philadelphia Brand cream cheese	¼ cup milk
	1 teaspoon onion salt

Combine ingredients, mixing until well blended. Chill. Serve with vegetable dippers or potato chips.

1-1/3 cups

Variations: Add any of the following to cream cheese mixture:

- 1/2 cup finely chopped ham and 2 teaspoons Kraft prepared horseradish
- 1/4 cup chopped stuffed green olives
- 4-oz. can mushrooms, drained, chopped, 2 tablespoons Kraft Italian dressing and 2 tablespoons Kraft grated parmesan cheese. Use as a dip or fill mushroom caps and broil until golden brown.

Tasty Crabmeat Canapés

1 8-oz. container soft Philadelphia Brand cream cheese	1 7½-oz. can crabmeat, drained, flaked
½ teaspoon lemon juice	¼ cup chopped radishes
¼ teaspoon onion salt	4 individual French bread loaves, baked, split
Dash of garlic salt	Parkay margarine
Dash of pepper	Chopped parsley

Combine cream cheese, lemon juice and seasonings, mixing until well blended. Add crabmeat and radishes; mix lightly. Spread bread halves with margarine. Top with crabmeat mixture; sprinkle with parsley. Cut diagonally into quarters.

32 appetizers

Sensational Stuffed Mushrooms

1 lb. medium mushrooms	½ cup (2 ozs.) Kraft grated
Parkay margarine	parmesan cheese
1 8-oz. container soft	2 tablespoons chopped
Philadelphia Brand	green onion
cream cheese	

Remove mushroom stems; chop enough stems to make 1/2 cup. Cook mushroom caps in margarine 5 minutes. Combine cream cheese and parmesan cheese, mixing until well blended. Add chopped stems and onion; mix well. Fill mushroom caps; broil until golden brown.

Approximately 2-1/2 dozen

Ham 'n Pickle Pinwheels

Boiled ham slices	Chopped pickle, parsley
Soft Philadelphia Brand	or onion
cream cheese	

For each appetizer, spread ham slice with cream cheese. Sprinkle with vegetable; roll up. Chill. Slice into 1/2-inch pieces.

Devilicious Ham Spread

A kids' favorite for toast or crackers. Make a supply for your active nibblers.

1 8-oz. container soft	1 teaspoon Kraft prepared
Philadelphia Brand	mustard
cream cheese	¼ teaspoon salt
1 2¼-oz. can deviled ham	Dash of pepper
1 tablespoon sweet pickle	
relish	

Combine cream cheese and deviled ham, mixing until well blended. Add remaining ingredients; mix well. Chill. Serve with party rye bread.

1-1/2 cups

Zucchini 'n Cheese Stuffed Celery

1 8-oz. container soft
   Philadelphia Brand
   cream cheese
¼ cup shredded zucchini
2 tablespoons chopped
   green onion

¼ teaspoon salt
   Celery, cut into 3-inch
   pieces
   Paprika, chili powder
   or ground red pepper

Combine cream cheese, zucchini, onion and salt, mixing until well blended. Fill celery with cream cheese mixture; sprinkle with paprika, chili powder or ground red pepper.

Lunch Meat Stack-Ups

8 luncheon meat slices
1 8-oz. container soft
   Philadelphia Brand
   cream cheese

Stuffed green olives
Pickle slices
Cherry tomatoes

For each stack-up, spread three meat slices with cream cheese. Stack slices; top with additional meat slice. Chill. Cut diagonally into quarters; cut each quarter in half. Top with olive, pickle or tomato; secure with picks. Serve on party rye bread or crackers, if desired.

16 appetizers

Zucchini Chive Dip

1 8-oz. container soft
   Philadelphia Brand
   cream cheese
3 tablespoons milk

1 small zucchini, shredded
3 tablespoons chopped
   chives
⅛ teaspoon salt

Combine cream cheese and milk, mixing until well blended. Add remaining ingredients; mix well. Chill. Serve with vegetable dippers or chips.

1 cup

Quick Wrap-Ups

10 **assorted luncheon meat
     slices**
 1 **8-oz. container soft
     Philadelphia Brand
     cream cheese**

10 **bread sticks**

For each wrap-up, spread one meat slice with cream cheese; wrap around bread stick.

10 appetizers

Nordic Style Tuna Paté

Prepare this molded spread well in advance and let the flavors mingle.

 1 **envelope unflavored gelatin**
 ¼ **cup cold water**
 2 **8-oz. containers soft
     Philadelphia Brand
     cream cheese**
 2 **6½-oz. cans tuna, drained,
     flaked**

 ½ **cup chopped celery**
 2 **tablespoons finely chopped
     onion**
 ½ **teaspoon dill weed**
 ½ **teaspoon lemon juice**
     Chopped parsley
     Cherry tomato halves

Soften gelatin in cold water; stir over low heat until dissolved. Combine cream cheese, tuna, celery, onion, dill weed and lemon juice, mixing until well blended. Gradually add gelatin mixture, mixing until blended. Pour into 1-quart bowl; chill until firm. Unmold onto serving plate; garnish with parsley and tomatoes. Serve with assorted crackers.

Chicken Tacos — page 30
Creamy Deviled Eggs — page 38
California Burgers — page 30

Chicken Tacos

1 8-oz. pkg. Philadelphia
   Brand cream cheese,
   cubed
⅓ cup milk
1½ cups chopped cooked
   chicken
1 4-oz. can chopped green
   chili peppers, drained

½ teaspoon salt
¼ teaspoon chili powder or
   ground cumin
10 taco shells
   Shredded lettuce
   Chopped tomato

Heat cream cheese and milk over low heat; stir until smooth. Stir in chicken, chili peppers and seasonings; heat thoroughly. Fill taco shells with meat mixture, lettuce and tomato.

10 tacos

California Burgers

1 8-oz. pkg. Philadelphia
   Brand cream cheese
1 medium avocado, peeled,
   mashed
1 tablespoon chopped onion
1 tablespoon lemon juice
½ teaspoon salt
½ cup chopped tomato
   *   *   *

2 lbs. ground beef
   Salt and pepper
6 Italian bread slices,
   toasted
   Lettuce
4 crisply cooked bacon
   slices, crumbled

Combine softened cream cheese, avocado, onion, lemon juice and salt, mixing until well blended. Add tomato; mix lightly.

Shape meat into six oval patties. Broil on both sides to desired doneness. Season with salt and pepper. For each sandwich, cover bread slice with lettuce, patty, cream cheese sauce and bacon.

6 sandwiches

Long Loaf Sandwich

A hot 'n hearty sausage sandwich that's great for casual entertaining — a meal-in-a-loaf.

1 lb. mild Italian sausage
½ cup chopped onion
½ cup chopped green pepper
1 4-oz. can mushrooms, drained
1 8-oz. pkg. Philadelphia Brand cream cheese, cubed
¼ cup (1 oz.) Kraft grated parmesan cheese
¼ cup water
¼ teaspoon oregano leaves, crushed
¼ teaspoon garlic salt
1 Italian bread loaf
1 6-oz. pkg. Kraft low moisture part-skim mozzarella cheese slices, cut in half

Remove sausage from casing. Brown sausage; drain. Add onion, green pepper and mushrooms; cook until tender. Add cream cheese, parmesan cheese, water and seasonings; stir over low heat until cream cheese is melted. Cut lengthwise slice from top of bread; scoop out center, leaving 1-inch shell. Place half of mozzarella cheese in shell; fill with meat mixture and remaining cheese. Cover with top bread slice. Place on ungreased cookie sheet. Bake at 400°, 10 minutes.

8 servings

"Philly" Fondue

1 8-oz. pkg. Philadelphia Brand cream cheese, cubed
¾ cup milk
1 cup (4 ozs.) shredded Kraft sharp cheddar cheese
¼ cup chopped green onion
French bread chunks

Heat cream cheese and milk in fondue pot or saucepan over low heat; stir until smooth. Add cheddar cheese; stir constantly until melted. Stir in onion. Dip bread chunks into fondue. Keep fondue hot while serving.

1-2/3 cups

Vegetable Pizza

Not the usual pizza — this strictly American version combines cream cheese, zucchini and mushrooms on a biscuit crust.

1 7½-oz. can refrigerated buttermilk biscuits
1 cup onion rings
1 cup chopped zucchini
1 4-oz. can mushrooms, drained

2 tablespoons Parkay margarine
1 8-oz. pkg. Philadelphia Brand cream cheese
¼ cup milk
1 egg
½ teaspoon salt

Separate each biscuit into two layers. Place in greased 12-inch pizza pan; press biscuits together to form crust. Sauté vegetables in margarine. Combine softened cream cheese, milk, egg and salt, mixing until well blended. Add vegetables; mix lightly. Pour over biscuit crust. Bake at 400°, 20 minutes, Serve immediately.

6 to 8 servings

"Philly" Sloppy Joes

A variation of a perennial favorite — sloppy joe sauce blended with cream cheese and spooned over cornbread.

1 lb. ground beef
½ cup chopped onion
½ cup chopped green pepper
¾ cup Kraft barbecue sauce
½ teaspoon salt

1 8-oz. pkg. Philadelphia Brand cream cheese, cubed
8 cornbread squares

Brown meat; drain. Add onion and green pepper; cook until tender. Stir in barbecue sauce and salt; simmer 15 minutes. Add cream cheese; stir over low heat until melted. For each sandwich, split cornbread square; cover halves with meat mixture.

8 sandwiches

Open-Face Denver Sandwiches

2 tablespoons chopped green pepper
2 tablespoons chopped onion
2 tablespoons Parkay margarine
6 eggs, beaten
½ cup chopped ham
¼ cup milk
½ teaspoon salt
Dash of pepper
1 8-oz. pkg. Philadelphia Brand cream cheese, cubed
3 English muffins, split, toasted

Sauté green pepper and onion in margarine. Add combined eggs, ham, milk and seasonings. Cook slowly, stirring occasionally until eggs begin to set. Add cream cheese; continue cooking, stirring occasionally, until cream cheese is melted and eggs are cooked. For each sandwich, cover muffin half with egg mixture.

6 sandwiches

Shrimpjohn Sandwiches

French bread generously topped with a piquant cream cheese spread and tender shrimp — how Parisian!

1 8-oz. pkg. Philadelphia Brand cream cheese
1 tablespoon milk
2 teaspoons lemon juice
1 tablespoon green onion slices
½ teaspoon Worcestershire sauce
Dash of salt and pepper
4 individual French bread loaves, baked, split or 4 English muffins, split, toasted
1 4½-oz. can shrimp, drained, rinsed
Chopped parsley

Combine softened cream cheese, milk and lemon juice, mixing until well blended. Add onion, Worcestershire sauce and seasonings; mix well. For each sandwich, spread both bread halves with cream cheese mixture. Top with shrimp; sprinkle with parsley.

4 sandwiches

Variation: Substitute eight 4-inch frozen fish sticks, cooked, for shrimp.

this

Savoy Sandwich

A terrific saucy sandwich for brunch, lunch or supper — surprise your family.

2 tablespoons chopped green pepper	Dash of pepper
2 tablespoons Parkay margarine	3 English muffins, split, toasted
4 eggs, beaten	6 Canadian-style bacon slices, cooked
¼ teaspoon salt	"Philly" Sauce Supreme

Sauté green pepper in margarine. Combine eggs and seasonings; pour into skillet. Cook slowly, stirring occasionally until eggs are cooked. For each sandwich, cover muffin half with bacon and scrambled eggs; top with:

"Philly" Sauce Supreme

1 8-oz. pkg. Philadelphia Brand cream cheese, cubed	¼ cup (1 oz.) Kraft grated parmesan cheese
½ cup milk	½ teaspoon onion salt

Heat cream cheese and milk over low heat; stir until smooth. Stir in remaining ingredients.

6 sandwiches

Empire Turkey Sandwich

1 8-oz. pkg. Philadelphia Brand cream cheese, cubed	¼ teaspoon salt
	¼ teaspoon garlic salt
1 cup milk	6 white bread slices, toasted
½ cup (2 ozs.) Kraft grated parmesan cheese	6 hot cooked turkey slices
	Paprika

Heat cream cheese and milk over low heat; stir until smooth. Stir in parmesan cheese and seasonings. For each sandwich, cover toast slice with turkey and cream cheese sauce; sprinkle with paprika.

6 sandwiches

Frosted Sandwich Loaf

A magnificent, do-ahead party loaf that's layered with egg and ham salads and frosted with cream cheese.

1 unsliced sandwich loaf	Dash of salt and pepper
Soft Parkay margarine	Egg Salad
2 8-oz. pkgs. Philadelphia	Ham Salad
Brand cream cheese	⅓ cup milk
¼ cup finely chopped	
watercress	

Trim crusts from bread. Cut into four lengthwise slices; spread with margarine. Combine 1/3 package softened cream cheese, watercress and seasonings, mixing until well blended. Spread one bread slice with Egg Salad, second slice with cream cheese mixture and third slice with Ham Salad. Stack layers; cover with fourth bread slice. Combine remaining softened cream cheese and milk, mixing until well blended. Frost sandwich loaf; chill.

Egg Salad

3 hard-cooked eggs, finely	¼ teaspoon salt
chopped	Dash of pepper
½ teaspoon Kraft prepared	Kraft mayonnaise
mustard	

Combine eggs, mustard, seasonings and enough mayonnaise to moisten; mix lightly.

Ham Salad

1 cup finely chopped ham	Kraft mayonnaise
2 tablespoons chopped sweet	
pickle	

Combine ham, pickle and enough mayonnaise to moisten; mix lightly.

12 servings.

"Philly" Club Sandwiches

A typical "club" with a special spread — cream cheese blended with bacon and onion.

1 8-oz. container soft Philadelphia Brand cream cheese	¼ cup chopped green onion
	12 white bread slices, toasted
	Cooked chicken slices
4 crisply cooked bacon slices, crumbled	Lettuce
	Tomato slices

Combine cream cheese, bacon and onion, mixing until well blended. For each sandwich, spread three toast slices with cream cheese mixture. Cover one toast slice with chicken, lettuce and second toast slice. Top with tomato and third toast slice. Cut into triangles; secure with picks.

4 sandwiches

Cheesy Beef Sandwiches

This savory sandwich filling can be kept several days in the refrigerator.

1 8-oz. container soft Philadelphia Brand cream cheese	1 2½-oz. pkg. smoked sliced beef, chopped
	¼ cup finely chopped onion
1 tablespoon milk	Dash of salt and pepper
	8 white bread slices

Combine cream cheese and milk, mixing until well blended. Add meat, onion and seasonings; mix well. For each sandwich, spread one bread slice with 1/3 cup cream cheese mixture; top with second bread slice.

4 sandwiches

Variations: Substitute 2½-oz. pkg. smoked sliced ham, chopped, for beef and finely chopped green pepper for onion.

Omit bread. Use cream cheese mixture as spread for crackers.

Bagel Toppers

Bagels, split, toasted
Soft Philadelphia Brand
cream cheese

Crisply cooked bacon
slices, crumbled
Hard-cooked eggs,
chopped

Spread bagels with cream cheese; top with bacon and egg.

Variations: Substitute any of the following for bacon and egg:

- Cucumber and onion slices
- Strawberry preserves
- Chopped radishes and shredded carrot
- Chopped stuffed green olives

Cucumber 'n Onion Sandwiches

1 8-oz. container soft
Philadelphia Brand
cream cheese
¼ cup chopped cucumber

¼ cup chopped onion
¼ teaspoon salt
Dash of garlic powder
8 whole-wheat bread slices

Combine cream cheese, vegetables and seasonings, mixing until well blended. For each sandwich, spread one bread slice with cream cheese mixture; top with second bread slice.

4 sandwiches

Sandwich Spread

A great spread for many breads — a make-ahead favorite for the family.

1 8-oz. container soft
Philadelphia Brand
cream cheese

¼ cup chopped stuffed
green olives
¼ cup chopped nuts

Combine cream cheese, olives and nuts, mixing until well blended. Serve with whole-wheat bread slices.

1-1/4 cups

Variation: Substitute 1/4 cup chopped dates for olives.

Cheesy Tuna Snacks

1 10-oz. can refrigerated big buttermilk flaky biscuits
1 8-oz. container soft Philadelphia Brand cream cheese

1 6½-oz. can tuna, drained, flaked
½ cup chopped celery
¼ cup sweet pickle relish
Dash of salt

Separate dough into ten biscuits. Make wide depression in center of each biscuit. Bake as directed on package. Combine remaining ingredients, mixing until well blended. Spoon approximately 1/4 cup cream cheese mixture into center of each biscuit.

10 servings

Snack Squares

1 8-oz. can refrigerated crescent dinner rolls
2 8-oz. containers soft Philadelphia Brand cream cheese

6 crisply cooked bacon slices, crumbled
¼ cup chopped green onion
2 tablespoons Kraft grated parmesan cheese

Separate dough into two long rectangles. Place in ungreased 13 × 9-inch baking pan; press onto bottom and 1/2-inch up sides to form crust. Bake at 375°, 15 to 20 minutes or until golden brown. Cool. Combine remaining ingredients, mixing until well blended. Spread over crust. Cut into squares.

32 appetizers

Creamy Deviled Eggs

8 hard-cooked eggs
1 8-oz. container soft Philadelphia Brand cream cheese

2 tablespoons sweet pickle relish
½ teaspoon dry mustard
¼ teaspoon salt
Dash of pepper

Cut eggs in half. Remove yolks; mash. Add remaining ingredients, mixing until well blended. Refill whites.

Garden Vegetable Spread

1 8-oz. container soft
   Philadelphia Brand
   cream cheese
½ cup shredded carrot
½ cup shredded zucchini

1 tablespoon chopped
   parsley
¼ teaspoon garlic salt
   Dash of pepper

Combine ingredients, mixing until well blended. Serve with bread slices or assorted crackers.

1-1/3 cups

Liver Sausage Snacks

1 8-oz. container soft
   Philadelphia Brand
   cream cheese
1 8-oz. pkg. liver sausage
2 tablespoons chopped
   green onioin

½ teaspoon Kraft prepared
   mustard
4 English muffins, split,
   toasted
   Tomato slices
   Sweet pickle slices

Combine cream cheese and liver sausage, mixing until well blended. Add onion and mustard; mix well. For each snack, spread muffin half with 1/4 cup cream cheese mixture; top with tomato and pickle.

8 servings

Pita Bread Sandwiches

1 8-oz. container soft
   Philadelphia Brand
   cream cheese
2 tablespoons milk
1 cup chopped cooked
   chicken
¼ cup chopped cucumber

¼ cup chopped onion
½ teaspoon salt
¼ teaspoon dill weed
⅛ teaspoon pepper
2 pita bread rounds,
   cut in half

Combine cream cheese and milk, mixing until well blended. Add chicken, cucumber, onion and seasonings; mix well. For each sandwich, fill pocket with 1/2 cup chicken mixture.

4 sandwiches

Bavarian Beef Sandwiches

1   8-oz. container soft   ¼   teaspoon salt
    Philadelphia Brand   6   rye bread slices
    cream cheese   Lettuce
¼   cup dairy sour cream   Roast beef slices
2   tablespoons Kraft prepared   6   red onion slices
    horseradish

Combine cream cheese, sour cream, horseradish and salt, mixing until well blended. For each sandwich, spread bread slice with cream cheese mixture. Cover with lettuce, meat, additional cream cheese mixture and onion.

6 sandwiches

Hawaiian Spread

1   8-oz. container soft   2   tablespoons Kraft apricot
    Philadelphia Brand   preserves
    cream cheese   ⅓   cup flaked coconut

Combine cream cheese and preserves, mixing until well blended. Add coconut; mix well. Chill. Serve with nut bread slices.

1-1/3 cups

Variations: Add 1/8 teaspoon anise seed.
            Substitute 1/4 cup whole berry cranberry sauce for preserves.
            Substitute Kraft pineapple or peach preserves for apricot preserves.

Majestic Spinach Salad — page 51
Pink Sparkle Freeze — page 42
Golden Fruit Dressing — page 42

Pink Sparkle Freeze

Served as a salad or dessert, this frozen fruit and honey combination is extra special for parties or family celebrations.

1 8-oz. pkg. Philadelphia
  Brand cream cheese
¼ cup honey
1 10-oz. pkg. frozen
  strawberries, thawed

1 8¼-oz. can crushed
  pineapple, undrained
1 cup whipping cream,
  whipped

Combine softened cream cheese and honey, mixing until well blended. Add fruit; mix lightly. Fold in whipped cream. Pour into 6-cup ring mold; freeze. Unmold; garnish with watercress, if desired.

6 to 8 servings

Variation: Substitute six 3/4-cup molds for ring mold.

Golden Fruit Dressing

1 8-oz. pkg. Philadelphia
  Brand cream cheese
¼ cup honey

¼ cup Kraft pasteurized
  orange juice
Dash of salt

Combine softened cream cheese, honey, orange juice and salt, mixing until well blended. Chill. Serve with fruit salads.

1-2/3 cups

Ginger-Orange Fruit Dressing

1 8-oz. pkg. Philadelphia
  Brand cream cheese
½ cup Kraft pasteurized
  orange juice

1 tablespoon sugar
¼ teaspoon ginger

Combine softened cream cheese and remaining ingredients, mixing until well blended. Chill. Serve with fruit.

1-1/2 cups

Roquefort Dressing Supreme

1 8-oz. pkg. Philadelphia Brand cream cheese
¾ cup (3 ozs.) roquefort cheese
¾ cup milk
¼ cup Kraft mayonnaise
3 tablespoons lemon juice
2 tablespoons chopped chives
1 teaspoon Worcestershire sauce
Dash of hot pepper sauce

Combine softened cream cheese and roquefort cheese, mixing until well blended. Add remaining ingredients; mix well. Chill. Serve with vegetable and meat salads.

2-1/2 cups

''Philly'' Waldorf Salad

1 8-oz. pkg. Philadelphia Brand cream cheese
2 tablespoons orange juice
1 tablespoon grated orange rind
1 tablespoon sugar
3 cups chopped apples
1 cup chopped celery
½ cup chopped pecans

Combine softened cream cheese, orange juice, orange rind and sugar, mixing until well blended. Add remaining ingredients; mix lightly. Chill.

8 servings

Sunny Fruit Salad

1 8-oz. pkg. Philadelphia Brand cream cheese
3 tablespoons milk
1 11-oz. can mandarin orange segments, drained
1 8¼-oz. can crushed pineapple, drained
1 cup grape halves
½ cup shredded coconut
¼ cup maraschino cherry halves

Combine softened cream cheese and milk, mixing until well blended. Add remaining ingredients; mix lightly. Chill several hours or overnight.

6 servings

Merry Cranberry Freeze

3 cups cranberries, ground or finely chopped
1½ cups sugar
1 8¼-oz. can crushed pineapple, drained
½ cup chopped walnuts
1 8-oz. pkg. Philadelphia Brand cream cheese
1 cup whipping cream, whipped

Combine cranberries and sugar. Add pineapple and nuts; mix well. Gradually add to softened cream cheese, mixing until well blended. Fold in whipped cream. Pour into 6-1/2-cup ring mold; freeze. Place in refrigerator 30 minutes before unmolding.

10 to 12 servings

Garden Macaroni Salad

2 cups (7 ozs.) elbow macaroni, cooked, drained
1 cup chopped cucumber
½ cup chopped green pepper
½ cup radish slices
2 tablespoons chopped onion
½ teaspoon salt
1 8-oz. pkg. Philadelphia Brand cream cheese
¼ cup Kraft mayonnaise
¼ cup sweet pickle relish
1 tablespoon Kraft prepared mustard

Combine macaroni, cucumber, green pepper, radishes, onion and salt; mix well. Combine softened cream cheese and remaining ingredients, mixing until well blended. Add to macaroni mixture; mix lightly. Spoon and gently press into lightly oiled 6-1/2-cup ring mold; chill several hours or overnight. Unmold onto serving plate. Garnish with cucumber slices and radish roses, if desired.

6 to 8 servings

Variation: Substitute lightly oiled 9-inch springform pan with ring insert for ring mold.

Garden Macaroni Salad

Unique Greek Salad

A complete meal in a salad — cubes of cream cheese replace feta cheese in this colorful mediterranean favorite.

6 tablespoons olive oil
2 tablespoons red wine vinegar
1 tablespoon chopped parsley
½ teaspoon sugar
Dash of salt and pepper
*   *   *
2 cups torn romaine
2 cups torn iceberg lettuce

1 8-oz. pkg. Philadelphia Brand cream cheese, cubed
1 cup red onion rings
1 medium cucumber, chopped
1 medium tomato, cut into wedges
¼ cup pitted ripe olives

Combine oil, vinegar, parsley, sugar and seasonings; mix well.

Combine remaining ingredients; toss lightly. Serve with dressing.

6 to 8 servings

Creamy Blue Cheese Salad

1 envelope unflavored gelatin
1 cup cold water
1 8-oz. pkg. Philadelphia Brand cream cheese

1 cup (4 ozs.) crumbled Kraft blue cheese
1 cup cottage cheese
¼ teaspoon onion salt
⅛ teaspoon celery salt
⅛ teaspoon paprika

Soften gelatin in 1/2 cup cold water; stir over low heat until dissolved. Add remaining cold water. Gradually add gelatin to combined softened cream cheese and remaining ingredients, mixing until well blended. Pour into lightly oiled 1-quart mold; chill until firm. Unmold.

8 to 10 servings

Zesty Potato Salad Ring

Surround this savory potato salad with cold meats and relishes and you have a flavorful and decorative centerpiece for a party buffet.

4 **cups chopped cooked potatoes**	2 **tablespoons chopped green onion**
½ **cup celery slices**	½ **teaspoon salt**
8 **crisply cooked bacon slices, crumbled**	⅓ **cup Kraft Italian dressing**
¼ **cup (1 oz.) Kraft grated parmesan cheese**	1 **8-oz. pkg. Philadelphia Brand cream cheese**

Combine potatoes, celery, bacon, parmesan cheese, onion and salt; mix lightly. Gradually add dressing to softened cream cheese, mixing until well blended. Pour over potato mixture; mix lightly. Spoon and gently press mixture into lightly oiled 4-1/2-cup ring mold; chill several hours or overnight. Unmold onto serving plate.

6 to 8 servings

Variation: Substitute lightly oiled 9-inch springform pan with ring insert for ring mold.

Orange Cream Squares

2 **3-oz. pkgs. orange flavored gelatin**	1 **8-oz. pkg. Philadelphia Brand cream cheese**
2 **cups boiling water**	2 **medium apples, chopped**
1 **cup cold water**	½ **cup chopped nuts**
	Lettuce

Dissolve gelatin in boiling water; add cold water. Gradually add to softened cream cheese, mixing until well blended. Chill until partially set; fold in apples and nuts. Pour into 8-inch square baking dish; chill until firm. Cut into squares; serve on lettuce-lined plates.

6 servings

Creamy Orange Salad

For a guest luncheon or brunch, serve this refreshing molded salad on an attractive platter with fresh fruit.

1 3-oz. pkg. orange flavored gelatin
1½ cups boiling water
1 8-oz. pkg. Philadelphia Brand cream cheese

¼ cup orange juice
1 tablespoon lemon juice
1 tablespoon grated orange rind

Dissolve gelatin in boiling water. Gradually add to softened cream cheese, mixing until well blended. Stir in juices and orange rind. Pour into lightly oiled 1-quart mold; chill until firm. Unmold; surround with lettuce, if desired.

4 to 6 servings

Emerald Isle Mold

A sparkling lime mold filled with grapefruit, apples and walnuts and topped with a cream cheese lime layer.

1 3-oz. pkg. lime flavored gelatin
1 cup boiling water
¾ cup cold water
1 8-oz. pkg. Philadelphia Brand cream cheese
    *   *   *
1 3-oz. pkg. lime flavored gelatin

1 cup boiling water
1 cup ginger ale
1 cup Kraft grapefruit sections, drained, cut in half
1 cup chopped apple
¼ cup chopped walnuts

Dissolve gelatin in boiling water; add cold water. Gradually add to softened cream cheese, mixing until well blended. Pour into lightly oiled 1-1/2-quart mold; chill until almost set.

Dissolve gelatin in boiling water; add ginger ale. Chill until partially set; fold in fruit and nuts. Pour over molded layer; chill until firm. Unmold.

6 to 8 servings

Frothy Lime Pear Mold

1 3-oz. pkg. lime flavored
   gelatin
1 cup boiling water
½ cup cold water
½ cup Kraft pasteurized
   orange juice
1 17-oz. can pear halves,
   drained

1 3-oz. pkg. lemon flavored
   gelatin
1 cup boiling water
¾ cup cold water
2 tablespoons lemon juice
1 8-oz. pkg. Philadelphia
   Brand cream cheese

    *   *   *

Dissolve lime gelatin in boiling water; add cold water and orange juice. Arrange pears on bottom of lightly oiled 6-cup ring mold; cover with gelatin. Chill until almost set.

Dissolve lemon gelatin in boiling water; add cold water and lemon juice. Gradually add to softened cream cheese, mixing until well blended. Pour over molded layer; chill until firm. Unmold.

6 to 8 servings

Imperial Peach Salad

1 17-oz. can peach slices,
   undrained
1 3-oz. pkg. cherry flavored
   gelatin
1 cup boiling water

1 3-oz. pkg. lemon flavored
   gelatin
1 cup boiling water
¾ cup cold water
1 8-oz. pkg. Philadelphia
   Brand cream cheese

    *   *   *

Drain peaches, reserving syrup. Dissolve cherry gelatin in boiling water; add reserved syrup and enough cold water to measure 1 cup. Chill until partially set. Arrange peaches on bottom of lightly oiled 6-cup ring mold; cover with gelatin. Chill until almost set.

Dissolve lemon gelatin in boiling water; add cold water. Gradually add to softened cream cheese, mixing until well blended. Pour over molded layer; chill until firm. Unmold; surround with lettuce, if desired.

6 to 8 servings

Festive Chicken Salad

1   8¼-oz. can crushed
    pineapple, undrained
1   8-oz. container soft
    Philadelphia Brand
    cream cheese
2   cups chopped cooked
    chicken
1   6-oz. can water chestnuts,
    drained, sliced

½   cup celery slices
¼   cup green onion slices
¼   cup slivered almonds,
    toasted
¼   teaspoon salt
    Dash of pepper
4   medium tomatoes

Drain pineapple, reserving syrup. Combine reserved syrup and cream cheese, mixing until well blended. Add pineapple and combined remaining ingredients; mix lightly. Chill. Cut each tomato into six sections, almost to stem end. Fill with chicken salad.

4 servings

Majestic Spinach Salad

The ingredients for this main dish salad can be layered and sealed for freshness with a savory cream cheese dressing then chilled overnight — a great time-saver.

1   cup (4 ozs.) Kraft Swiss
    cheese, cubed
1   qt. torn spinach
4   hard-cooked eggs, sliced
2   cups mushroom slices
1   8-oz. container soft
    Philadelphia Brand
    cream cheese

½   cup dairy sour cream
3   tablespoons milk
2   teaspoons lemon juice
2   teaspoons sugar
¼   cup green onion slices
4   crisply cooked bacon
    slices, crumbled

In 2-quart bowl, layer Swiss cheese, spinach, eggs and mushrooms. Combine cream cheese, sour cream, milk, lemon juice and sugar, mixing until well blended. Stir in green onion. Spread over salad to seal. Cover; chill several hours or overnight. Top with bacon before serving.

6 to 8 servings

Festive Chicken Salad

Hearty Egg Salad

1 8-oz. container soft Philadelphia Brand cream cheese	8 hard-cooked eggs, chopped
⅓ cup Miracle Whip salad dressing	½ cup chopped celery
2 tablespoons sweet pickle relish	2 tablespoons green onion slices
	Dash of salt and pepper
	Lettuce

Combine cream cheese, salad dressing and pickle relish, mixing until well blended. Add remaining ingredients; mix lightly. Chill. Serve on lettuce-lined plates.

6 to 8 servings

Variations: For sandwiches, fill bread slices with egg salad and lettuce.

Cut six tomatoes into six sections each, almost to stem end. Fill with egg salad.

Molded Salmon Salad

1 envelope unflavored gelatin	¼ teaspoon salt
¾ cup cold water	1 7¾-oz. can salmon, drained, flaked
1 8-oz. container soft Philadelphia Brand cream cheese	½ cup finely chopped celery
¼ cup Kraft mayonnaise	2 tablespoons chopped parsley
1 tablespoon lemon juice	

Soften gelatin in cold water; stir over low heat until dissolved. Cool. Gradually add gelatin to combined cream cheese, mayonnaise, lemon juice and salt, mixing until well blended. Stir in remaining ingredients; mix lightly. Pour into lightly oiled 3-cup mold; chill until firm. Unmold; Garnish with additional chopped parsley and lemon slices, if desired.

4 to 6 servings

Frosted Pineapple Salad

2 8¼-oz. cans pineapple
    chunks, undrained
2 3-oz. pkgs. cherry flavored
    gelatin
2 cups boiling water

Cold water
1 8-oz. container soft
    Philadelphia Brand
    cream cheese

Drain pineapple, reserving syrup. Dissolve gelatin in boiling water; add reserved syrup and enough cold water to measure 2 cups. Reserve 2 tablespoons gelatin mixture. Chill remaining gelatin until partially set; fold in fruit. Pour into 8-inch square baking dish; chill until almost set. Gradually add reserved gelatin to cream cheese, mixing until well blended. Spread over molded layer; chill until firm.

6 to 8 servings

Molded Fruit Salad

1 8¼-oz. can crushed
    pineapple, undrained
1 3-oz. pkg. lemon flavored
    gelatin
1 cup boiling water

Cold water
1 8-oz. container soft
    Philadelphia Brand
    cream cheese
1 medium apple, chopped

Drain pineapple, reserving syrup. Dissolve gelatin in boiling water; add reserved syrup and enough cold water to measure 1/2 cup. Gradually add to cream cheese, mixing until well blended. Chill until partially set; fold in fruit. Pour into 8-inch square baking dish; chill until firm.

6 to 8 servings

Perfection Vegetable Mold

A crisp carrot slaw molded in creamy orange gelatin — a flavorful accompaniment salad for any meal.

1 8¼-oz. can crushed
   pineapple, undrained
1 3-oz. pkg. orange flavored
   gelatin
½ cup boiling water

1 8-oz. container soft
   Philadelphia Brand
   cream cheese
1 cup shredded cabbage
½ cup shredded carrot
½ cup celery slices

Drain pineapple, reserving syrup. Dissolve gelatin in boiling water; add reserved syrup and enough cold water to measure 1/2 cup. Gradually add to cream cheese, mixing until well blended. Fold in remaining ingredients. Pour into lightly oiled 1-quart mold; chill until firm. Unmold.

4 to 6 servings

Fruit Slaw

1 20-oz. can crushed
   pineapple, well-drained
1 8-oz. container soft
   Philadelphia Brand
   cream cheese

3 cups shredded cabbage
1 cup chopped celery
1 cup chopped apple
½ cup chopped nuts

Combine pineapple and cream cheese, mixing until well blended. Add combined remaining ingredients; toss lightly. Chill.

10 to 12 servings

Variation: Substitute 1 cup green grape halves or 11-oz. can mandarin orange segments, drained, for apple.

Zippy Zucchini Mold

1 envelope unflavored
  gelatin
¼ cup cold water
1 8-oz. container soft
  Philadelphia Brand
  cream cheese
½ cup dairy sour cream

1 cup shredded zucchini
¼ cup chopped green
  onion
2 tablespoons chopped green
  chili peppers
¼ teaspoon salt
  Dash of garlic powder

Soften gelatin in cold water; stir over low heat until dissolved. Cool. Gradually add gelatin to combined cream cheese and sour cream, mixing until well blended. Add remaining ingredients; mix well. Pour into lightly oiled 3-cup mold; chill until firm. Unmold.

4 to 6 servings

Avocado Cream Dressing

1 8-oz. container soft
  Philadelphia Brand
  cream cheese
1 medium avocado, peeled,
  mashed
⅓ cup milk

4 crisply cooked bacon
  slices, crumbled
1 tablespoon finely chopped
  onion
2 teaspoons lemon juice

Combine ingredients, mixing until well blended. Chill. Serve with assorted greens.

2 cups

Garlic Cheese Dressing

1 8-oz. container soft
  Philadelphia Brand
  cream cheese
½ cup dairy sour cream

¼ cup milk
1 teaspoon lemon juice
1 garlic clove, minced
  Dash of salt and pepper

Combine ingredients, mixing until well blended. Chill. Serve with vegetable and main dish salads.

1-2/3 cups

"Philly" Parm Dressing

1 8-oz. container soft
    Philadelphia Brand
    cream cheese
½ cup milk
¼ cup (1 oz.) Kraft grated
    parmesan cheese

1 tablespoon chopped
    parsley
1 tablespoon chopped green
    onion
1 teaspoon lemon juice

Combine ingredients, mixing until well blended. Chill. Serve with green salads.

1-2/3 cups

Sour Cream Fruit Dressing

1 8-oz. container soft
    Philadelphia Brand
    cream cheese
½ cup dairy sour cream

2 tablespoons sugar
2 tablespoons orange juice
1 teaspoon grated orange
    rind

Combine ingredients, mixing until well blended. Chill. Serve with fruit salads.

1-1/2 cups

Poppy Seed Dressing

A sweet-sour dressing made in minutes with soft cream cheese.

1 8-oz. container soft
    Philadelphia Brand
    cream cheese
¼ cup milk

2 tablespoons sugar
2 tablespoons poppy seeds
1 teaspoon vinegar

Combine ingredients, mixing until well blended. Chill. Serve with citrus or spinach salads.

1-1/3 cups

Zucchini Bisque — page 58
Sandwich Sauce Superb — page 68

Zucchini Bisque

2 cups chopped zucchini
1 cup water
½ cup tomato juice
1 tablespoon chopped onion
1 chicken bouillon cube

⅛ teaspoon basil leaves
1 8-oz. pkg. Philadelphia
  Brand cream cheese,
  cubed

In saucepan, combine all ingredients except cream cheese. Bring to boil. Cover; simmer 20 minutes. Pour into blender container. Add cream cheese; blend until smooth. Return to saucepan; heat thoroughly.

Six 1/2-cup servings

Broccoli Soup

For a special luncheon or light supper, serve this hearty cream cheese soup with a ham or chicken sandwich.

¼ cup chopped onion
1 tablespoon Parkay
  margarine
1 8-oz. pkg. Philadelphia
  Brand cream cheese,
  cubed
1 cup milk
1 chicken bouillon cube

¾ cup boiling water
1 10-oz. pkg. frozen
  chopped broccoli,
  cooked, drained
½ teaspoon lemon juice
½ teaspoon salt
  Dash of pepper
  Slivered almonds, toasted

Sauté onion in margarine. Add cream cheese and milk; stir over low heat until cream cheese is melted. Dissolve bouillon in boiling water; add to cream cheese mixture. Stir in broccoli, lemon juice and seasonings; heat thoroughly. Top each serving with nuts.

Six 1/2-cup servings

Variation: Substitute 10-oz. pkg. frozen chopped spinach, cooked, drained, for broccoli.

Corny Cheese Soup

⅓ cup chopped green pepper
¼ cup chopped onion
2 tablespoons Parkay margarine
1 8-oz. pkg. Philadelphia Brand cream cheese, cubed

1 cup milk
1 chicken bouillon cube
1 cup boiling water
1 8¾-oz. can cream style corn
½ teaspoon salt
Dash of pepper

Sauté green pepper and onion in margarine. Add cream cheese and milk; stir over low heat until cream cheese is melted. Dissolve bouillon in boiling water; add to cream cheese mixture. Stir in remaining ingredients; heat thoroughly.

Four 1-cup servings

Creme Vichyssoise

A cream cheese version of a famous French appetizer soup. Traditionally served chilled, it is also delicious warm.

4 cups chicken broth or bouillon
4 cups chopped potatoes
¼ cup onion slices
1½ teaspoons salt

1 8-oz. pkg. Philadelphia Brand cream cheese
1 tablespoon finely chopped chives

In large saucepan, combine broth, potatoes, onion and salt; bring to boil. Cover; simmer 20 minutes or until potatoes are very tender. Force mixture through sieve. Gradually add to softened cream cheese, mixing until well blended. Stir in chives. Chill. Garnish with additional chives, if desired.

Twelve 1/2-cup servings

Double Cheese Soup

Cheddar and cream cheese in the same soup — superb!
Serve it as an appetizer or for lunch with a crisp green salad.

¼ cup chopped onion
1 tablespoon Parkay margarine
1 8-oz. pkg. Philadelphia Brand cream cheese, cubed
1 cup milk

1 cup (4 ozs.) shredded Kraft sharp cheddar cheese
1 cup water
2 tablespoons chopped parsley

Sauté onion in margarine. Add cream cheese and milk; stir over low heat until cream cheese is melted. Add cheddar cheese; stir until melted. Stir in water and parsley; heat thoroughly. Garnish each serving with croutons, if desired.

Six 1/2-cup servings

Florentine Soup

½ cup mushroom slices
½ cup chopped onion
2 tablespoons Parkay margarine
1 tablespoon flour
1 teaspoon salt
¼ teaspoon garlic salt
Dash of pepper

3½ cups milk
1 10-oz. pkg. frozen chopped spinach, cooked, drained
1 8-oz. pkg. Philadelphia Brand cream cheese, cubed

Sauté mushrooms and onion in margarine. Blend in flour and seasonings. Gradually add milk; cook, stirring constantly, until thickened. Add remaining ingredients; stir over low heat until cream cheese is melted.

Six 1-cup servings

Variations: Soup may also be chilled and served cold.
Top servings with crisply cooked bacon, crumbled or croutons.
Serve soup chilled.

Potato Potage

A savory potato soup for lunch or supper — the perfect companion for crisp vegetable or fruit salads.

½ cup celery slices
¼ cup chopped onion
2 tablespoons Parkay margarine
1 8-oz. pkg. Philadelphia Brand cream cheese, cubed
1 cup milk

2 cups chopped cooked potatoes
½ cup water
2 tablespoons Kraft grated parmesan cheese
½ teaspoon dry mustard
½ teaspoon salt
Dash of pepper

Sauté celery and onion in margarine. Add cream cheese and milk; stir over low heat until cream cheese is melted. Stir in remaining ingredients; heat thoroughly.

Eight 1/2-cup servings

Lemon Egg Soup

Reminiscent of the Greek avgolemeno soup, this refreshing version features cream cheese. Serve small portions as appetizers and heartier amounts for luncheon.

2 10¾-oz. cans condensed chicken broth
½ cup rice
1 8-oz. pkg. Philadelphia Brand cream cheese

2 eggs
2 tablespoons lemon juice
½ teaspoon grated lemon rind

Bring broth to boil; add rice. Cover; simmer 20 minutes. Remove from heat. Combine softened cream cheese, eggs and lemon juice, mixing until well blended. Gradually add to broth; stir constantly until smooth. Stir in lemon rind; heat thoroughly.

Eight 1/2-cup servings

Onion Cheese Soup

2 cups onion rings
1 tablespoon Parkay
   margarine

1 8-oz. pkg. Philadelphia
   Brand cream cheese,
   cubed
2 beef bouillon cubes
1½ cups boiling water

Sauté onion in margarine. Add cream cheese; stir over low heat until cream cheese is melted. Dissolve bouillon in boiling water; add to cream cheese mixture. Heat thoroughly.

Six 1/2-cup servings

Savory Mushroom Soup

3 cups mushroom slices
¼ cup finely chopped onion
2 tablespoons Parkay
   margarine
1 cup milk

1 8-oz. pkg. Philadelphia
   Brand cream cheese,
   cubed
1 beef bouillon cube
½ cup boiling water

Sauté mushrooms and onion in margarine. Add milk and cream cheese; stir over low heat until cream cheese is melted. Dissolve bouillon in boiling water; add to cream cheese mixture. Heat thoroughly.

Six 1/2-cup servings

Jubilee Sauce

1 8-oz. pkg. Philadelphia
   Brand cream cheese
½ cup dairy sour cream

¼ cup Kraft pasteurized
   orange juice
¼ cup sugar

Combine softened cream cheese and remaining ingredients, mixing until well blended. Chill. Serve over fruit compotes, apple crisp or fruit pies.

2 cups

Chiffon Dessert Sauce

A fluffy chiffon sauce flavored with vanilla — delicious over warm baked puddings, spicy cakes or fresh berries.

1 8-oz. pkg. Philadelphia Brand cream cheese	2 eggs, separated
¼ cup sugar	1½ teaspoons vanilla

Combine softened cream cheese, sugar, egg yolks and vanilla, mixing until well blended. Fold in stiffly beaten egg whites. Serve over upside-down cake or gingerbread.

2 cups

"Philly" Hard Sauce

A winter holiday tradition that retains its popularity throughout the year. For variety, substitute vanilla or brandy flavoring.

1 8-oz. pkg. Philadelphia Brand cream cheese	1½ cups sifted confectioners' sugar
	1 teaspoon rum flavoring

Combine softened cream cheese, sugar and flavoring, mixing until well blended. Serve over date nut bread, plum pudding or fruit cake.

2/3 cup

Sauce Louis

1 8-oz. pkg. Philadelphia Brand cream cheese, cubed	¼ teaspoon Kraft prepared horseradish
¼ cup milk	¼ teaspoon salt
½ cup chili sauce	Dash of ground red pepper
½ teaspoon Worcestershire sauce	

Heat cream cheese and milk over low heat; stir until smooth. Stir in remaining ingredients. Chill. Serve over shrimp, cold vegetables or hard-cooked eggs.

1-1/2 cups

"Philly" Chocolate Sauce

Transform simple desserts into something extra special with this versatile cream cheese chocolate sauce.

1 8-oz. pkg. Philadelphia Brand cream cheese, cubed
⅓ cup milk

2 1-oz. squares unsweetened chocolate
2 cups sifted confectioners' sugar
1 teaspoon vanilla

Heat cream cheese, milk and chocolate over low heat; stir until smooth. Stir in remaining ingredients. Serve over poached pears or ice cream.

2 cups

Note: This sauce can be refrigerated and then reheated.

Chive Sauce

1 8-oz. pkg. Philadelphia Brand cream cheese, cubed
½ cup milk

1 tablespoon chopped chives
1 teaspoon lemon juice
¼ teaspoon garlic salt

Heat cream cheese and milk over low heat; stir until smooth. Stir in remaining ingredients. Serve over hot cooked potatoes, green beans, broccoli or asparagus.

1-1/3 cups

Delmonico Sauce

1 8-oz. pkg. Philadelphia Brand cream cheese, cubed
½ cup milk

¼ cup (1 oz.) Kraft cold pack blue cheese, crumbled
Dash of onion salt

Heat cream cheese and milk over low heat; stir until smooth. Stir in remaining ingredients. Serve over hot cooked vegetables. Top with additional blue cheese, if desired.

1-1/4 cups

"Philly" Chocolate Sauce

Parisian Wine Sauce

1 8-oz. pkg. Philadelphia Brand cream cheese, cubed
⅓ cup milk
2 tablespoons dry white wine
1 tablespoon green onion slices
¼ teaspoon salt
Dash of ground red pepper

Heat cream cheese and milk over low heat; stir until smooth. Stir in remaining ingredients. Serve over fish, chicken or pork.

1-1/3 cups

Regal Cheese Sauce

1 8-oz. pkg. Philadelphia Brand cream cheese, cubed
½ cup milk
¼ cup (1 oz.) Kraft grated parmesan cheese
¼ teaspoon garlic salt

Heat cream cheese and milk over low heat; stir until smooth. Stir in remaining ingredients. Serve over hot cooked vegetables.

1-3/4 cups

Philadelphia Hollandaise

This marvelous sauce is delicious over eggs benedict or hot ham sandwiches.

1 8-oz. pkg. Philadelphia Brand cream cheese, cubed
½ cup milk
2 egg yolks
2 tablespoons lemon juice
Dash of salt

Heat cream cheese and milk over low heat; stir until smooth. Blend in egg yolks, lemon juice and salt. Serve over hot cooked vegetables.

1-3/4 cups

Dill Sauce

1 8-oz. pkg. Philadelphia
  Brand cream cheese,
  cubed
⅓ cup milk
½ teaspoon dill weed

¼ teaspoon lemon juice
¼ teaspoon salt
  Dash of ground red
  pepper

Heat cream cheese and milk over low heat; stir until smooth. Stir in remaining ingredients. Serve over omelets or hot cooked vegetables.

1-1/3 cups

Epicurean Sauce

1 8-oz. pkg. Philadelphia
  Brand cream cheese,
  cubed
¼ cup milk
2 tablespoons Parkay
  margarine
¼ cup dry white wine

2 tablespoons chopped
  parsley
2 tablespoons finely chopped
  onion
¼ teaspoon salt
  Dash of pepper

Heat cream cheese, milk and margarine over low heat; stir until smooth. Stir in remaining ingredients; heat thoroughly. Serve over meat or fish.

1-1/2 cups

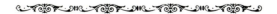

Sandwich Sauce Superb

1 8-oz. container soft
  Philadelphia Brand
  cream cheese
¼ cup Kraft mayonnaise
3 tablespoons milk

¼ teaspoon Kraft prepared
  mustard
1 hard-cooked egg, chopped
1 tablespoon chopped green
  onion
  Dash of pepper

Combine cream cheese, mayonnaise, milk and mustard, mixing until well blended. Add remaining ingredients; mix lightly. Chill. Serve over cold sandwiches.

1-1/3 cups

Horseradish Sauce

1 8-oz. container soft
  Philadelphia Brand
  cream cheese
2 tablespoons milk

1 tablespoon chopped green
  onion
2 teaspoons Kraft prepared
  horseradish

Combine ingredients, mixing until well blended. Serve over meat or sandwiches.

1 cup

Tangy Tartar Sauce

Quick, easy and piquant — a perfect sauce for almost any seafood.

1 8-oz. container soft
  Philadelphia Brand
  cream cheese
2 tablespoons milk
1 teaspoon Kraft prepared
  mustard
2 tablespoons chopped
  green onion

2 tablespoons chopped sweet
  pickle
2 tablespoons chopped
  stuffed green olives
¼ teaspoon salt
  Dash of pepper

Combine cream cheese, milk and mustard, mixing until well blended. Add remaining ingredients; mix well. Chill. Stir before serving. Serve over fish.

1-1/4 cups

Sweet 'n Sour Sauce

1 8-oz. container soft
   Philadelphia Brand
   cream cheese
½ cup dairy sour cream

¼ cup milk
2 tablespoons sugar
1 tablespoon vinegar
   Dash of salt

Combine ingredients, mixing until well blended. Serve over cold ham sandwiches or fruit.

2 cups

Heavenly Dessert Sauce

1 8-oz. container soft
   Philadelphia Brand
   cream cheese

3 tablespoons sugar
3 tablespoons milk
½ teaspoon vanilla

Combine ingredients, mixing until well blended. Serve over fruit or pound cake.

1-1/2 cups

Variations: Substitute 1 tablespoon lemon juice, 1 teaspoon grated lemon rind and dash of nutmeg for vanilla. Substitute 1/4 cup orange juice and 2 teaspoons grated orange rind for milk and vanilla.

Honey Date Sauce

Soft cream cheese blends beautifully with other ingredients for this honey of a sauce.

1 8-oz. container soft
   Philadelphia Brand
   cream cheese
¼ cup milk

¼ cup chopped dates
2 tablespoons honey
1 teaspoon lemon juice
   Dash of cinnamon

Combine ingredients, mixing until well blended. Chill. Serve over pound cake or baked apples.

1-1/3 cups

Lemon Cream Topping

1 8-oz. container soft Philadelphia Brand cream cheese	2 tablespoons milk
	1 tablespoon lemon juice
¼ cup sifted confectioners' sugar	1 teaspoon grated lemon rind

Combine ingredients, mixing until well blended. Serve over gingerbread or fruit.

1-1/3 cups

Spicy Apple Sauce

1 8-oz. container soft Philadelphia Brand cream cheese	1 tablespoon sugar
	1 teaspoon lemon juice
¼ cup applesauce	Dash of salt
1 tablespoon milk	Dash of cinnamon

Combine ingredients, mixing until well blended. Chill. Stir before serving. Serve over ice cream or gingerbread squares.

1-1/2 cups

Toasted Almond Sauce

1 8-oz. container soft Philadelphia Brand cream cheese	1 tablespoon milk
	2 tablespoons chopped almonds, toasted
2 tablespoons Kraft orange marmalade	1 tablespoon sugar
	Dash of salt

Combine cream cheese, marmalade and milk, mixing until well blended. Add remaining ingredients; mix well. Chill. Serve over pound cake.

1-1/4 cups

Stuffed Squash — page 72
Vegetable Stir-Fry — page 72

Stuffed Squash

A hearty vegetable for chilly winter days — special enough for guests.

¼ cup slivered almonds
1 tablespoon Parkay margarine
1 8-oz. pkg. Philadelphia Brand cream cheese, cubed
¾ cup milk
1 10-oz. pkg. frozen cut green beans, cooked, drained
½ cup water chestnuts, sliced
1½ teaspoons lemon juice
½ teaspoon ginger
½ teaspoon dry mustard
¼ teaspoon salt
2 acorn squash, cut in half, baked

In saucepan, sauté nuts in margarine until lightly browned. Add cream cheese and milk; stir over low heat until cream cheese is melted. Stir in remaining ingredients except squash; heat thoroughly. Spoon vegetable mixture into hot baked squash.

4 servings

Vegetable Stir-Fry

Stir-frying retains the bright colors and crisp texture of fresh vegetables.

2 cups diagonally cut carrot slices
2 cups diagonally cut celery slices
¾ cup thin green pepper strips
2 tablespoons Parkay margarine
¼ teaspoon salt
Dash of pepper
1 8-oz. pkg. Philadelphia Brand cream cheese, cubed
¼ cup sesame seeds, toasted

Stir-fry vegetables in margarine until crisp-tender. Add seasonings; mix lightly. Remove from heat. Coat cream cheese cubes with sesame seeds. Add to vegetables; mix lightly.

6 to 8 servings

Country Corn Casserole

1 8-oz. pkg. Philadelphia
   Brand cream cheese
2 eggs
1 12-oz. can whole kernel
   corn, drained

1 medium carrot, shredded
¼ cup chopped green onion
¼ cup chopped green pepper
¼ teaspoon salt
   Dash of pepper

Combine softened cream cheese and eggs, mixing until well blended. Add remaining ingredients; mix well. Pour into lightly greased 8-inch square baking dish. Bake at 350°, 40 minutes.

4 servings

Cream Cheese Kugel

1 8-oz. pkg. Philadelphia
   Brand cream cheese
¼ cup Parkay margarine,
   melted
4 eggs, slightly beaten
½ cup milk

¼ cup sugar
1½ teaspoons salt
4 cups (8 ozs.) noodles,
   cooked, drained
½ cup raisins

Combine softened cream cheese and margarine, mixing until well blended. Blend in eggs, milk, sugar and salt. Add noodles and raisins; mix well. Pour into 11-3/4 × 7-1/2-inch baking dish. Bake at 375°, 30 to 35 minutes or until set.

6 to 8 servings

Savory Spinach Casserole

1 8-oz. pkg. Philadelphia
   Brand cream cheese
¼ cup milk

2 10-oz. pkgs. frozen
   chopped spinach,
   cooked, drained
⅓ cup Kraft grated parmesan
   cheese

Combine softened cream cheese and milk, mixing until well blended. Place spinach in 1-quart casserole; top with cream cheese mixture. Sprinkle with parmesan cheese. Bake at 350°, 20 minutes.

4 to 6 servings

Creamy Cabbage

6 cups shredded cabbage
½ cup chopped onion
½ cup water
1 8-oz. pkg. Philadelphia Brand cream cheese, cubed

½ teaspoon celery seed
½ teaspoon salt
Dash of pepper

Combine cabbage, onion and water; bring to boil. Cover; simmer 10 minutes or until cabbage is crisp-tender. Add remaining ingredients; stir over low heat until cream cheese is melted.

6 servings

Mixed Vegetable Bake

1 8-oz. pkg. Philadelphia Brand cream cheese, cubed
½ cup milk
1 10-oz. pkg. frozen mixed vegetables, cooked, drained

¼ teaspoon salt
Dash of pepper
1 cup hot mashed potatoes
1 small tomato, sliced

Heat cream cheese and milk over low heat; stir until smooth. Add mixed vegetables and seasonings; mix well. Pour into 1-quart casserole. Cover with potatoes; top with tomato slices. Bake at 350°, 20 minutes.

4 servings

Savory Rice

1 8-oz. pkg. Philadelphia Brand cream cheese, cubed
½ cup water
2 cups hot cooked rice

4 crisply cooked bacon slices, crumbled
2 tablespoons green onion slices
Dash of salt and pepper

Heat cream cheese and water over low heat; stir until smooth. Stir in remaining ingredients; heat thoroughly.

4 to 6 servings

Piquant Broccoli

1 8-oz. pkg. Philadelphia
   Brand cream cheese,
   cubed
¼ cup Miracle Whip salad
   dressing
¼ cup milk

⅓ cup chopped green pepper
¼ cup chopped pimiento
2 tablespoons chopped onion
2 10-oz. pkgs. frozen
   broccoli spears, cooked,
   drained

Heat cream cheese, salad dressing and milk over low heat; stir until smooth. Stir in green pepper, pimiento and onion; heat thoroughly. Serve over hot broccoli.

4 to 6 servings

Regal Rice Ring

A hint of lemon, a creamy sauce and a few choice vegetables make this ring party perfect.

1 cup thin celery slices
¼ cup chopped green onion
1 tablespoon Parkay
   margarine
1 8-oz. pkg. Philadelphia
   Brand cream cheese,
   cubed
¼ cup milk
1 egg

3 cups hot cooked rice
1 teaspoon lemon juice
1 teaspoon salt
⅛ teaspoon pepper
2 teaspoons dry bread
   crumbs
1 10-oz. pkg. frozen peas,
   cooked, drained

Sauté celery and onion in margarine. Add cream cheese and milk; stir over low heat until cream cheese is melted. Remove from heat. Blend in egg. Add rice, lemon juice and seasonings; mix well. Sprinkle lightly greased 6-cup ring mold with crumbs. Press rice mixture into mold. Bake at 350°, 15 minutes. Cool 10 minutes. Unmold onto serving plate; fill center with hot peas.

6 servings

Sweet Potato Casserole

A unique combination — sweet potatoes, pineapple, pecans and cream cheese with a touch of nutmeg.

1 8¼-oz. can pineapple chunks, undrained
½ cup Kraft pasteurized orange juice
1 8-oz. pkg. Philadelphia Brand cream cheese, cubed
⅛ teaspoon nutmeg
Dash of salt
2 17-oz. cans sweet potatoes, drained, sliced
Chopped pecans

Drain pineapple, reserving syrup. Add enough water to syrup to measure 1/2 cup. Add syrup, orange juice and seasonings to cream cheese; stir over low heat until smooth. Add sweet potatoes, pineapple and 1/4 cup nuts; mix lightly. Spoon into 1-1/2-quart casserole; sprinkle with additional nuts. Bake at 350°, 15 to 20 minutes or until hot.

6 servings

Potato Puff Extraordinaire

For family or friends this creamy puff is something special. Serve it hot from the oven, like a soufflé.

4 cups hot mashed potatoes
1 8-oz. pkg. Philadelphia Brand cream cheese
⅓ cup finely chopped onion
¼ cup chopped pimiento
1 egg, beaten
1 teaspoon salt
Dash of pepper

Combine potatoes and softened cream cheese, mixing until well blended. Add remaining ingredients; mix well. Spoon into 1-1/2-quart casserole. Bake at 350°, 40 minutes. Serve immediately.

6 to 8 servings

Variations: Substitute chopped green pepper for onion.
Sprinkle with crisply cooked bacon, crumbled.

Party Potato Bake

A savory casserole that resembles scalloped potatoes — cream cheese makes the difference.

2 bacon slices, chopped	**1 cup milk**
½ cup chopped onion	**1 teaspoon salt**
½ cup chopped green pepper	**⅛ teaspoon pepper**
1 8-oz. pkg. Philadelphia Brand cream cheese, cubed	**4 cups thinly sliced potatoes**

Fry bacon until crisp; remove from skillet. Drain fat, reserving 1 tablespoon. Sauté onion and green pepper in fat. Add cream cheese, milk and seasonings; stir over low heat until cream cheese is melted. Add potatoes; mix lightly. Spoon into 10 × 6-inch baking dish; sprinkle with bacon. Bake at 350°, 50 to 55 minutes or until potatoes are tender.

6 servings

Asparagus Delmonico

An elegant accompaniment for baked ham, cornish hens or steak.

1 8-oz. pkg. Philadelphia Brand cream cheese, cubed	**Dash of onion salt**
½ cup milk	**2 10-oz. pkgs. frozen asparagus spears, cooked, drained**
¼ cup (1 oz.) Kraft cold pack blue cheese, crumbled	

Heat cream cheese and milk over low heat; stir until smooth. Stir in blue cheese and onion salt. Serve over hot asparagus. Top with additional blue cheese, if desired.

4 to 6 servings

Spinach Treat

1 8-oz. pkg. Philadelphia
  Brand cream cheese,
  cubed
2 tablespoons Parkay
  margarine
2 tablespoons milk

¼ teaspoon hot pepper sauce
2 10-oz. pkgs. frozen
  chopped spinach, cooked,
  drained
1 hard-cooked egg, finely
  chopped

Heat cream cheese, margarine, milk and hot pepper sauce over low heat; stir until smooth. Stir in spinach; heat thoroughly. Garnish with egg.

4 to 6 servings

Sensational Saucy Noodles

½ cup chopped onion
1 tablespoon Parkay
  margarine
1 8-oz. pkg. Philadelphia
  Brand cream cheese,
  cubed
½ cup dairy sour cream

½ cup milk
1 10-oz. pkg. frozen peas,
  cooked, drained
1 teaspoon lemon juice
½ teaspoon salt
2 cups (4 ozs.) noodles,
  cooked, drained

Sauté onion in margarine. Add cream cheese, sour cream and milk; stir over low heat until cream cheese is melted. Add peas, lemon juice and salt; mix well. Combine cream cheese mixture and hot noodles; mix lightly.

4 to 6 servings

Main Dish Popover — page 81
Garden Fresh Stroganoff — page 80

Main Dish Popover

The batter puffs high around the savory creamed ground beef filling as the casserole bakes.

½ lb. ground beef
½ cup chopped onion
1 8-oz. pkg. Philadelphia Brand cream cheese, cubed
¼ cup water
½ teaspoon salt
½ teaspoon oregano leaves, crushed

¼ teaspoon ground cumin
*   *   *
2 eggs, beaten
¾ cup flour
½ teaspoon salt
¾ cup milk
1 tablespoon cornmeal
1 medium tomato, chopped

Brown meat; drain. Add onion; cook until tender. Add cream cheese and water; stir over low heat until cream cheese is melted. Stir in seasonings.

Combine eggs, flour, salt and milk; beat until smooth. Pour into greased 9-inch pie plate; sprinkle with cornmeal. Spoon meat mixture over batter. Bake at 400°, 35 minutes. Top with tomato.

6 to 8 servings

Variation: Add 4-oz. can chopped green chili peppers, drained, to meat mixture.

Sunday Brunch

¼ lb. bulk pork sausage
½ cup chopped onion
8 eggs, beaten
½ cup milk
¼ teaspoon salt

Dash of pepper
1 8-oz. pkg. Philadelphia Brand cream cheese, cubed

Brown sausage; drain. Add onion; cook until tender. Add combined eggs, milk and seasonings; cook slowly, stirring until eggs begin to set. Add cream cheese; continue cooking, stirring occasionally, until cream cheese is melted and eggs are cooked.

6 servings

Garden Fresh Stroganoff

1 lb. round steak, cut into strips
1 tablespoon Parkay margarine
1 small green pepper, cut into strips
½ cup water
1 cup mushroom slices
1 medium tomato, cut into wedges

1 8-oz. pkg. Philadelphia Brand cream cheese, cubed
¾ cup milk
¼ cup green onion slices
1 tablespoon sherry
½ teaspoon onion salt
Hot cooked noodles

*   *   *

Brown meat in margarine. Add green pepper and water; mix lightly. Cover; cook over medium heat 10 minutes or until meat is tender. Stir in mushrooms and tomato; continue cooking 10 minutes.

Heat cream cheese and milk over low heat; stir until smooth. Stir in onion, sherry and onion salt; heat thoroughly. Spoon meat mixture over noodles; top with cream cheese sauce. Garnish with additional green onion slices, if desired.

4 to 6 servings

Savory Scrambled Eggs

2 tablespoons Parkay margarine
6 eggs, beaten
⅓ cup milk

Salt and pepper
1 3-oz. pkg. Philadelphia Brand cream cheese, cubed

Melt margarine in skillet over low heat. Add combined eggs, milk and seasonings; cook slowly, stirring until eggs begin to set. Add cream cheese; continue cooking, stirring occasionally, until cream cheese is melted and eggs are cooked. Serve with toast and sprinkle with paprika, if desired.

4 servings

Variation: Add chopped parsley, chives, green onion slices or crisply cooked bacon, crumbled, as eggs begin to set.

Beefy Supper Treat

¼ cup chopped onion
1 tablespoon Parkay margarine
1 8-oz. pkg. Philadelphia Brand cream cheese, cubed
¾ cup milk
1 2½-oz. pkg. smoked sliced beef, chopped
1 4-oz. can mushrooms, drained
¼ cup (1 oz.) Kraft grated parmesan cheese
2 tablespoons chopped parsley
6 white bread slices, toasted, cut in half diagonally

Sauté onion in margarine. Add cream cheese and milk; stir over low heat until cream cheese is melted. Stir in meat, mushrooms, parmesan cheese and parsley; heat thoroughly. Serve over toast triangles.

6 servings

Variation: Substitute 1 lb. browned round steak, cut into strips, for smoked sliced beef. Serve in patty shells.

Winner's Spaghetti

½ cup chopped green pepper
⅓ cup chopped onion
1 tablespoon Parkay margarine
1 8-oz. pkg. Philadelphia Brand cream cheese, cubed
¼ cup milk
1 pkg. Kraft spaghetti with meat sauce dinner
1 3½-oz. can French fried onions

Sauté vegetables in margarine. Add cream cheese and milk; stir over low heat until cream cheese is melted. Prepare spaghetti as directed on package; combine with half of meat sauce. In 10 × 6-inch baking dish, layer spaghetti mixture, cream cheese mixture and remaining Meat Sauce; sprinkle with the Grated Parmesan Cheese. Bake at 350°, 25 minutes. Top with onions; continue baking 5 minutes.

6 servings

Chicken a la Ring

Creamed chicken in a crust made easy with convenient refrigerated dough.

1 **8-oz. pkg. Philadelphia Brand cream cheese**	2 **tablespoons chopped pimiento**
¼ **cup Miracle Whip salad dressing**	½ **teaspoon salt**
	¼ **teaspoon pepper**
3 **cups chopped cooked chicken**	2 **8-oz. cans refrigerated crescent dinner rolls**
¼ **cup chopped onion**	* * *
¼ **cup celery slices**	
¼ **cup slivered almonds, toasted**	1 **10¾-oz. can condensed cream of celery soup**
	⅓ **cup milk**

Combine softened cream cheese and salad dressing, mixing until well blended. Add chicken, vegetables, nuts, pimiento and seasonings; mix lightly. Separate dough into eight rectangles; firmly press perforations to seal. Press six rectangles over bottom and up sides of 6-cup ring mold to form crust. Spoon chicken mixture into crust. Cut each remaining rectangle crosswise into four strips; place over chicken mixture. Seal edges to enclose filling. Bake at 325°, 1 hour. Cool 10 minutes; invert onto serving platter.

Combine soup and milk; heat thoroughly. Serve with chicken ring.

8 servings

Variation: Substitute 9-inch springform pan with ring insert for 6-cup ring mold.

Corny Beef Bake

Serve this southwestern-style casserole with a fresh fruit salad for a hearty economical meal.

1 lb. ground beef	1 8¾-oz. can cream style
½ cup chopped onion	corn
⅓ cup chopped green pepper	* * *
1 6-oz. can tomato paste	½ cup cornmeal
½ cup water	½ cup flour
½ teaspoon salt	2 teaspoons baking powder
1 8-oz. pkg. Philadelphia	¼ teaspoon salt
Brand cream cheese	⅓ cup milk
1 egg	2 tablespoons Parkay
	margarine, melted
	1 egg

Brown meat; drain. Add onion and green pepper; cook until tender. Stir in tomato paste, water and salt; simmer 5 minutes. Spoon into 9-inch square baking dish. Combine softened cream cheese and egg, mixing until well blended. Add corn; mix lightly. Spoon over meat mixture.

Combine dry ingredients. Add combined milk, margarine and egg, mixing just until moistened. Spoon over cream cheese mixture. Bake at 400°, 30 to 35 minutes or until golden brown. Let stand 5 minutes before serving.

6 to 8 servings

Simple Supper

1 lb. ground beef	½ teaspoon salt
½ cup chopped onion	Dash of pepper
1 10¾-oz. can condensed	1 8-oz. pkg. Philadelphia
cream of mushroom soup	Brand cream cheese,
½ teaspoon paprika	cubed

Brown meat; drain. Add onion; cook until tender. Stir in soup and seasonings; simmer 15 minutes, stirring occasionally. Add cream cheese; stir until melted. Serve over toast or hot cooked noodles.

4 to 6 servings

Ham 'n Pineapple Casserole

A hearty ham, pineapple and noodle casserole. Serve with a crisp spinach salad and freshly baked muffins or rolls.

1 **8-oz. pkg. Philadelphia Brand cream cheese, cubed**	½ **cup celery slices**
¾ **cup milk**	2 **teaspoons Worcestershire sauce**
2 **cups finely chopped ham**	½ **teaspoon salt**
2 **cups (4 ozs.) noodles, cooked, drained**	**Dash of pepper**
1 **8¼-oz. can crushed pineapple, drained**	¼ **cup dry bread crumbs**
	1 **tablespoon Parkay margarine, melted**

Heat cream cheese and milk over low heat; stir until smooth. Add remaining ingredients except bread crumbs and margarine; mix well. Pour into 1-1/2-quart casserole. Top with bread crumbs tossed with margarine. Bake at 350°, 55 minutes.

6 servings

Beef 'n Corn Casserole

1 **lb. ground beef**	1 **12-oz. can whole kernel corn, drained**
½ **cup chopped onion**	¼ **cup chopped pimiento**
1 **10¾-oz. can condensed cream of mushroom soup**	¼ **teaspoon salt**
1 **8-oz. pkg. Philadelphia Brand cream cheese, cubed**	**Dash of pepper**
	1 **7½-oz. can refrigerated buttermilk biscuits**

Brown meat; drain. Add onion; cook until tender. Add soup and cream cheese; stir over low heat until cream cheese is melted. Add corn, pimiento and seasonings; mix lightly. Pour into 1-1/2-quart casserole. Separate dough into ten biscuits; cut each in half crosswise. Place biscuits, cut side down, around edge of casserole. Bake at 375°, 20 to 25 minutes or until biscuits are browned.

6 servings

"Philly" Brunch Quiche

The Americanization of a French favorite! A unique quiche made with cream cheese and seasoned with dill.

1 8-oz. pkg. Philadelphia Brand cream cheese, cubed
1 cup milk
¼ cup chopped onion
1 tablespoon Parkay margarine

4 eggs, beaten
1 cup finely chopped ham
¼ cup chopped pimiento
¼ teaspoon dill weed
Dash of pepper
1 10-inch unbaked pastry shell

Heat cream cheese and milk over low heat; stir until smooth. Sauté onion in margarine. Gradually add cream cheese sauce to eggs. Add onion, ham, pimiento and seasonings; mix well. Pour into pastry shell. Bake at 350°, 35 to 40 minutes or until set. Garnish with ham and fresh dill, if desired.

8 servings

Spinach Mushroom Bake

1½ cups chopped mushrooms
3 tablespoons Parkay margarine
½ cup crushed buttery crackers
¼ cup (1 oz.) Kraft grated parmesan cheese
        *   *   *

1 8-oz. pkg. Philadelphia Brand cream cheese
2 eggs
1 10-oz. pkg. frozen chopped spinach, cooked, drained
1 teaspoon lemon juice
1 teaspoon onion salt
Dash of pepper

Sauté mushrooms in margarine. Combine with crackers and parmesan cheese; press onto bottom of 10 × 6-inch baking dish.

Combine softened cream cheese and eggs, mixing until well blended. Add remaining ingredients; mix well. Pour over crust. Bake at 350°, 35 to 40 minutes or until set.

4 to 6 servings

"Philly" Brunch Quiche

Country Casserole

1½ cups milk
1 8-oz. pkg. Philadelphia Brand cream cheese, cubed
1 10-oz. pkg. frozen peas, cooked, drained
7 ozs. spaghetti, cooked, drained
1 6½-oz. can tuna, drained, flaked
1 4-oz. can mushrooms, drained
¼ cup (1 oz.) Kraft grated parmesan cheese
1 tablespoon chopped pimiento
1 tablespoon chopped onion
½ teaspoon onion salt
¼ teaspoon oregano leaves, crushed

Heat milk and cream cheese over low heat; stir until smooth. Add remaining ingredients; mix well. Pour into 2-quart casserole. Bake at 350°, 20 minutes.

6 to 8 servings

Sicilian Supper

1 lb. ground beef
½ cup chopped onion
1 6-oz. can tomato paste
¾ cup water
1 teaspoon salt
⅛ teaspoon garlic powder
        *   *   *
½ cup chopped green pepper
1 tablespoon Parkay margarine
1 8-oz. pkg. Philadelphia Brand cream cheese, cubed
¾ cup milk
2 cups (4 ozs.) noodles, cooked, drained
⅓ cup Kraft grated parmesan cheese
¼ teaspoon salt

Brown meat; drain. Add onion; cook until tender. Stir in tomato paste, water, salt and garlic powder; simmer 5 minutes.

Sauté green pepper in margarine. Add cream cheese and milk; stir over low heat until cream cheese is melted. Add noodles, parmesan cheese and salt; mix lightly. In 10 × 6-inch baking dish, arrange alternate crosswise rows of meat mixture and noodles. Bake at 350°, 20 minutes.

6 to 8 servings

Creamy Turkey Tetrazzini

½ cup chopped onion
½ cup chopped celery
¼ cup Parkay margarine
1 10¾-oz. can chicken broth
1 8-oz. pkg. Philadelphia Brand cream cheese, cubed
7 ozs. spaghetti, cooked, drained
1 cup chopped cooked turkey
1 4-oz. can mushrooms, drained
2 tablespoons chopped pimiento
¼ teaspoon salt
¼ cup (1 oz.) Kraft grated parmesan cheese

Sauté onion and celery in margarine. Add broth and cream cheese; stir over low heat until cream cheese is melted. Add remaining ingredients except parmesan cheese; mix lightly. Pour into 1-1/2-quart casserole; sprinkle with parmesan cheese. Bake at 350°, 30 minutes.

6 servings

Ham and Cheese Bake

Something special for family or friends — ham and broccoli baked in a mustard seasoned cream cheese sauce.

12 white bread slices, crusts trimmed
1½ cups (6 ozs.) shredded Kraft sharp cheddar cheese
1 10-oz. pkg. frozen chopped broccoli, cooked, drained
1 cup chopped ham
1 8-oz. pkg. Philadelphia Brand cream cheese
3 eggs
1 cup milk
½ teaspoon dry mustard
½ teaspoon salt

Place six bread slices on bottom of 11-3/4 × 7-1/2-inch baking dish. Cover with 1 cup cheddar cheese, broccoli, ham and remaining bread slices, cut diagonally in half. Combine softened cream cheese and eggs, mixing until well blended. Blend in milk and seasonings; pour over bread. Top with remaining cheddar cheese. Bake at 350°, 45 to 50 minutes or until set. Let stand 10 minutes before serving.

6 servings

Gloucester Halibut

2 12-oz. pkgs. frozen halibut
   steaks, thawed
Salt and pepper

¼ cup Parkay margarine,
   melted
1 tablespoon lemon juice
   "Philly" Tartar Sauce

Place fish in greased 11-3/4 × 7-1/2-inch baking dish; season with salt and pepper. Combine margarine and lemon juice; pour over fish. Bake at 450°, 20 minutes or until fish flakes easily with fork. Serve with:

"Philly" Tartar Sauce

1 8-oz. pkg. Philadelphia
   Brand cream cheese
⅓ cup Kraft mayonnaise
2 tablespoons milk

2 teaspoons sweet pickle
   relish
1 teaspoon finely chopped
   onion
½ teaspoon chopped capers

Combine softened cream cheese and remaining ingredients, mixing until well blended.

4 to 6 servings

Tuna Broccoli Bake

2 6½-oz. cans tuna, drained,
   flaked
1½ cups cooked rice
1 10-oz. pkg. frozen
   chopped broccoli,
   cooked, drained
½ cup chopped onion
2 tablespoons chopped
   pimiento

½ teaspoon salt
   Dash of pepper
1 8-oz. pkg. Philadelphia
   Brand cream cheese,
   cubed
¼ cup milk
¼ cup (1 oz.) Kraft grated
   parmesan cheese

Combine tuna, rice, broccoli, onion, pimiento and seasonings; mix lightly. Heat cream cheese and milk over low heat; stir until smooth. Stir in parmesan cheese. Add to tuna mixture; mix well. Spoon into 10 × 6-inch baking dish. Bake at 350°, 40 minutes.

6 to 8 servings

Chicken Potato Bake

1 12-oz. pkg. frozen
   shredded hash brown
   potatoes, thawed, drained
½ teaspoon salt
1 tablespoon Parkay
   margarine

    *   *   *

1 cup celery slices
½ cup chopped carrots
¼ cup chopped onion
2 tablespoons Parkay
   margarine

1 8-oz. pkg. Philadelphia
   Brand cream cheese,
   cubed
¾ cup milk
2 cups chopped cooked
   chicken
1 teaspoon lemon juice
½ teaspoon salt
¼ teaspoon poultry seasoning
   Dash of pepper

Combine potatoes and salt; mix lightly. Press onto bottom of 10 × 6-inch baking dish greased with margarine. Bake at 425°, 30 minutes. Reduce oven temperature to 350°.

Sauté vegetables in margarine. Add cream cheese and milk; stir over low heat until cream cheese is melted. Add remaining ingredients; mix well. Spoon mixture over potatoes. Bake at 350°, 30 minutes.

6 to 8 servings

Italian Spaghetti

¼ lb. mushrooms, sliced
1 medium green pepper,
   chopped
¼ cup chopped onion
¼ cup Kraft Italian dressing
1 8-oz. pkg. Philadelphia
   Brand cream cheese,
   cubed
1 cup milk

½ cup (2 ozs.) shredded Kraft
   low moisture part-skim
   mozzarella cheese
¼ cup (1 oz.) Kraft grated
   parmesan cheese
7 ozs. spaghetti, cooked,
   drained
6 crisply cooked bacon
   slices, crumbled

Sauté vegetables in dressing. Add cream cheese, milk and mozzarella cheese; stir over low heat until cheese is melted. Stir in parmesan cheese. Pour over combined hot spaghetti and bacon. Sprinkle with additional parmesan cheese, if desired.

6 servings

Meatball Stroganoff

1 lb. ground beef
⅓ cup dry bread crumbs
⅓ cup milk
1 egg, beaten
½ teaspoon Worcestershire
   sauce
1 teaspoon salt
   Dash of pepper
¼ cup oil

2 tablespoons green onion
   slices
1 8-oz. pkg. Philadelphia
   Brand cream cheese,
   cubed
¾ cup water
1 4-oz. can mushrooms,
   drained
4 cups (8 ozs.) noodles,
   cooked, drained

Combine meat, crumbs, milk, egg, Worcestershire sauce and seasonings; mix lightly. Shape into twenty-four meatballs. Brown in oil; continue cooking 10 to 15 minutes or until done. Remove meatballs; drain fat, reserving 1 tablespoon. Add onion; cook until tender. Add cream cheese, water and mushrooms; stir over low heat until cream cheese is melted. Spoon meatballs over hot noodles; top with cream cheese sauce. Garnish with additional green onion slices, if desired.

6 to 8 servings

Florentine Macaroni Bake

1 7¼-oz. pkg. Kraft
   macaroni and cheese
   dinner
1 8-oz. pkg. Philadelphia
   Brand cream cheese,
   cubed

1 10-oz. pkg. frozen chopped
   spinach, cooked, drained
6 crisply cooked bacon
   slices, crumbled
2 eggs, beaten
¼ teaspoon salt
   Dash of pepper

Prepare Dinner as directed on package, omitting margarine. Add cream cheese; stir over low heat until melted. Add remaining ingredients; mix well. Pour into 9-inch springform pan. Bake at 350°, 30 minutes. Let stand 5 minutes before serving.

6 servings

Philadelphia Nut Bread — page 94
Brandied-Cherry Coffee Cake — page 94
Treasure Bran Muffins — page 95

Philadelphia Nut Bread

1 8-oz. pkg. Philadelphia
   Brand cream cheese
⅓ cup granulated sugar
1 egg
     *   *   *
2¼ cups flour
 ⅓ cup granulated sugar
 ⅓ cup packed brown sugar

1 teaspoon baking soda
1 teaspoon salt
½ cup oil
½ cup milk
2 eggs
1 teaspoon grated lemon
   rind
1 cup chopped nuts

Combine softened cream cheese, granulated sugar and egg, mixing until well blended.

Combine dry ingredients. Add combined oil, milk, eggs and lemon rind, mixing just until moistened. Fold in nuts. Spread 1 cup batter into greased 9-inch springform pan with ring insert. Top with cream cheese mixture; cover with remaining batter. Bake at 350°, 1 hour. Cool 10 minutes; remove from pan. Invert onto serving plate.

Variation: Substitute greased 9 × 5-inch loaf pan for springform pan.

Brandied-Cherry Coffee Cake

1 8-oz. pkg. Philadelphia
   Brand cream cheese
1 cup sugar
½ cup Parkay margarine
2 eggs
1 teaspoon vanilla
1¾ cups flour
1 teaspoon baking powder

½ teaspoon baking soda
¼ teaspoon salt
¼ cup milk
1 21-oz. can cherry pie
   filling
1 tablespoon brandy
¼ cup sliced almonds

Combine softened cream cheese, sugar and margarine, mixing until well blended. Blend in eggs and vanilla. Add combined dry ingredients alternately with milk, mixing well after each addition. Pour into greased and floured 13 × 9-inch baking pan. Combine pie filling and brandy; spoon over batter. Sprinkle with nuts. Bake at 350°, 1 hour.

Treasure Bran Muffins

The "treasure" is the sweet cream cheese filling.

1¼ cups bran cereal	½ teaspoon salt
1 cup milk	½ cup raisins
¼ cup oil	* * *
1 egg	1 8-oz. pkg. Philadelphia
1¼ cups flour	Brand cream cheese
½ cup sugar	¼ cup sugar
1 tablespoon baking powder	1 egg

Combine cereal and milk; let stand 2 minutes. Add oil and egg; mix well. Add combined dry ingredients, mixing just until moistened. Fold in raisins. Spoon into greased and floured medium-size muffin pan, filling each cup 2/3 full.

Combine softened cream cheese, sugar and egg, mixing until well blended. Drop rounded tablespoonfuls cream cheese mixture onto batter. Bake at 375°, 25 minutes.

1 dozen

Apple Kuchen

2 cups all-purpose biscuit mix	¼ cup sugar
	1 egg
⅔ cup milk	¼ teaspoon vanilla
¼ cup sugar	1½ cups thin peeled
2 tablespoons oil	apple slices
1 egg	* * *
* * *	3 tablespoons sugar
1 8-oz. pkg. Philadelphia	¼ teaspoon cinnamon
Brand cream cheese	

Combine biscuit mix, milk, sugar, oil and egg; mix well. Pour into greased and floured 13 × 9-inch baking pan.

Combine softened cream cheese, sugar, egg and vanilla, mixing until well blended. Spread cream cheese mixture over batter; top with apples.

Combine sugar and cinnamon; sprinkle over apples. Bake at 350°, 35 to 40 minutes.

Crullers

1 **8-oz. pkg. Philadelphia Brand cream cheese**	1 **cup flour**
⅓ **cup Parkay margarine**	**Dash of salt**
	Sugar

Combine softened cream cheese and margarine, mixing until well blended. Add flour and salt; mix well. Shape dough into ball; chill 1 hour. On lightly floured surface, roll out dough to 12 × 6-inch rectangle. Cut dough into twenty-four 1/2-inch strips. Fry in deep hot oil, 375°, 1 minute or until golden brown, turning once. Drain on absorbent paper. Roll in sugar.

Approximately 2 dozen

Pull Apart Ring

1 **8-oz. pkg. Philadelphia Brand cream cheese**	⅓ **cup chopped nuts**
½ **cup granulated sugar**	* * *
1 **tablespoon grated orange rind**	½ **cup sifted confectioners' sugar**
2 **8-oz. cans refrigerated crescent dinner rolls**	1 **tablespoon milk**

Combine softened cream cheese, granulated sugar and orange rind, mixing until well blended. For each can of rolls, separate dough into two long rectangles. Overlap long sides to form 13 × 7-inch rectangle; firmly press perforations and edges to seal. Spread with half of cream cheese mixture; sprinkle with half of nuts. Roll up from long end; seal long end. Cut each roll into nine slices. Place 6-oz. custard cup in center of greased cookie sheet. Arrange six rolls in ring around cup. Arrange remaining rolls in ring around first six. Bake at 375°, 25 to 30 minutes or until golden brown. Cool; remove cup. Loosen ring from cookie sheet. Invert onto cooling rack, then again onto serving plate.

Combine confectioners' sugar and milk; mix well. Drizzle over ring.

Blueberries 'n Cheese Coffee Cake

Fresh blueberries, nuggets of cream cheese and a sugar crusted top are the special features of this splendid cake.

1¼ cups sugar
½ cup Parkay margarine
2 eggs
2¼ cups flour
1 tablespoon baking powder
1 teaspoon salt
¾ cup milk
¼ cup water
2 cups fresh blueberries
1 8-oz. pkg. Philadelphia Brand cream cheese, cubed

1 teaspoon grated lemon rind

*   *   *

¼ cup sugar
¼ cup flour
1 teaspoon grated lemon rind
2 tablespoons Parkay margarine

Cream sugar and margarine until light and fluffy. Blend in eggs. Combine 2 cups flour, baking powder and salt. Add to creamed mixture alternately with milk and water, mixing well after each addition. Toss blueberries with 1/4 cup flour; fold into batter with cream cheese and lemon rind. Pour into greased and floured 13 × 9-inch baking pan.

Combine sugar, flour and lemon rind; cut in margarine until mixture resembles coarse crumbs. Sprinkle over batter. Bake at 375°, 1 hour.

Variation: Substitute 2 cups frozen blueberries, thawed, drained, for fresh blueberries.

Chocolate Ripple Coffee Cake

1 8-oz. pkg. Philadelphia
   Brand cream cheese
⅓ cup sugar
1 egg
1 6-oz. pkg. semi-sweet
   chocolate pieces
½ teaspoon vanilla
   *   *   *
1 8-oz. pkg. Philadelphia
   Brand cream cheese

1 cup sugar
½ cup Parkay margarine
2 eggs
½ teaspoon vanilla
1¾ cups flour
1 teaspoon baking powder
½ teaspoon baking soda
¼ teaspoon salt
½ cup milk

Combine softened cream cheese, sugar and egg, mixing until well blended. Stir in chocolate pieces and vanilla.

Combine softened cream cheese, sugar and margarine, mixing until well blended. Blend in eggs and vanilla. Add combined dry ingredients alternately with milk, mixing well after each addition. Spoon half of batter into greased and floured 10-inch tube pan. Top with cream cheese mixture; cover with remaining batter. Bake at 350°, 1 hour. Cool 10 minutes; remove from pan.

Berry Patch Coffee Cake

1 8-oz. pkg. Philadelphia
   Brand cream cheese
1 cup sugar
½ cup Parkay margarine
2 eggs
½ teaspoon vanilla
2 cups sifted cake flour

1 teaspoon baking powder
½ teaspoon baking soda
¼ teaspoon salt
¼ cup milk
½ cup Kraft red raspberry
   preserves

Combine softened cream cheese, sugar and margarine, mixing until well blended. Blend in eggs and vanilla. Add combined dry ingredients alternately with milk, mixing well after each addition. Pour into greased and floured 13 × 9-inch baking pan. Dot with preserves; cut through batter with knife several times for marble effect. Bake at 350°, 35 minutes.

Favorite Banana Bread

1 8-oz. pkg. Philadelphia
  Brand cream cheese
1 cup sugar
¼ cup Parkay margarine
1 cup mashed banana

2 eggs
2¼ cups flour
1½ teaspoons baking powder
½ teaspoon baking soda
1 cup chopped nuts

Combine softened cream cheese, sugar and margarine, mixing until well blended. Blend in banana and eggs. Add combined dry ingredients, mixing just until moistened. Fold in nuts. Pour into greased and floured 9 × 5-inch loaf pan. Bake at 350°, 1 hour and 10 minutes. Cool 10 minutes; remove from pan.

Variation: Substitute greased and floured 9-inch springform pan with ring insert for loaf pan. Bake at 350°, 1 hour.

Raisin Scones

1 8-oz. pkg. Philadelphia
  Brand cream cheese
½ cup sugar
⅓ cup raisins
1 teaspoon grated lemon
  rind
      *   *   *

3 cups flour
1 tablespoon baking powder
1½ teaspoons salt
½ cup Parkay margarine
1 cup milk
  Honey

Combine softened cream cheese and sugar, mixing until well blended. Add raisins and lemon rind; mix well.

Combine dry ingredients; cut in margarine until mixture resembles coarse crumbs. Add milk, mixing just until moistened. Divide dough in half. On lightly floured surface, roll out each half to 12 × 9-inch rectangle. Spread one rectangle with cream cheese mixture; top with remaining dough. Cut into twelve 3-inch squares; cut each square in half diagonally. Place on ungreased cookie sheet. Bake at 425°, 12 to 15 minutes or until lightly browned. Drizzle with honey.

2 dozen

Pumpkin Cheese Bread

2½ cups sugar
1 8-oz. pkg. Philadelphia Brand cream cheese
½ cup Parkay margarine
4 eggs
1 16-oz. can pumpkin
3½ cups flour

2 teaspoons baking soda
1 teaspoon salt
1 teaspoon cinnamon
½ teaspoon baking powder
¼ teaspoon ground cloves
1 cup chopped nuts

Combine sugar, softened cream cheese and margarine, mixing until well blended. Add eggs, one at a time, mixing well after each addition. Blend in pumpkin. Add combined dry ingredients, mixing just until moistened. Fold in nuts. Pour into two greased and floured 9 × 5-inch loaf pans. Bake at 350°, 1 hour and 10 minutes or until wooden pick inserted in center comes out clean. Cool 10 minutes; remove from pans.

2 loaves

''Philly'' Brunch Cake

⅓ cup packed brown sugar
⅓ cup flour
½ teaspoon cinnamon
2 tablespoons Parkay margarine
        *   *   *
1¼ cups granulated sugar
1 8-oz. pkg. Philadelphia Brand cream cheese

½ cup Parkay margarine
2 eggs
1 teaspoon vanilla
1¾ cups flour
1 teaspoon baking powder
½ teaspoon baking soda
¼ teaspoon salt
¼ cup milk

Combine dry ingredients; cut in margarine until mixture resembles coarse crumbs.

Combine granulated sugar, softened cream cheese and margarine, mixing until well blended. Blend in eggs and vanilla. Add combined dry ingredients alternately with milk, mixing well after each addition. Pour into greased and floured 13 × 9-inch baking pan. Sprinkle with crumb mixture. Bake at 350°, 35 to 40 minutes or until wooden pick inserted in center comes out clean.

Pumpkin Cheese Bread

Glazed Sweet Rolls

¾ cup milk
Parkay margarine
1 teaspoon lemon juice
3½ to 4 cups flour
½ cup granulated sugar
2 pkgs. active dry yeast
½ teaspoon salt
3 eggs
½ cup chopped nuts
*   *   *

1 8-oz. pkg. Philadelphia
Brand cream cheese
¼ cup granulated sugar
1 teaspoon lemon juice
1 egg, separated
*   *   *
1¾ cups sifted confectioners'
sugar
3 tablespoons milk

Heat milk and 1/2 cup margarine over low heat until warm. Stir in lemon juice. Add to combined 2 cups flour, granulated sugar, yeast and salt; beat 2 minutes at medium speed on electric mixer. Add eggs; beat 2 minutes. Stir in enough remaining flour to form a soft dough. On lightly floured surface, knead dough until smooth and elastic, about 5 minutes. Place in greased bowl; brush with melted margarine. Cover; let rise in warm place until double in volume, about 1-1/2 hours. Punch down dough. On lightly floured surface, roll out dough to 18 × 12-inch rectangle; sprinkle with nuts. Roll up from long end; seal long end. Cut into eighteen 3/4-inch slices. Place 1 inch apart on greased cookie sheet; flatten to 4-inch circle. Cover; let rise until double in volume, about 45 minutes.

Combine softened cream cheese, granulated sugar and lemon juice, mixing until well blended. Blend in egg yolk. Make depression in center of each roll; fill with rounded tablespoonful cream cheese mixture. Brush dough with beaten egg white. Bake at 350°, 15 minutes.

Combine confectioners' sugar and milk; mix well. Drizzle over warm rolls.

1-1/2 dozen

Make Ahead: Prepare as directed. Cover; refrigerate. When ready to serve, reheat loosely wrapped in foil at 350°, 15 minutes.

Kolacky

A rich, sweet roll of European origin especially popular in the Midwest where there are large settlements of Poles, Czechoslovakians and Bohemians.

¾ **cup milk**
Parkay margarine
4½ **to 4¾ cups flour**
½ **cup sugar**
2 **pkgs. active dry yeast**

1 **teaspoon salt**
3 **eggs**
½ **teaspoon grated lemon rind**
Cream Cheese Filling

Heat milk and 1/2 cup margarine over low heat until warm. Add to combined 1 cup flour, sugar, yeast and salt; beat 2 minutes at medium speed on electric mixer. Add 1/2 cup flour, eggs and lemon rind; beat 2 minutes. Stir in enough remaining flour to form a soft dough. On lightly floured surface, knead dough until smooth and elastic, about 5 minutes. Place in greased bowl; brush with melted margarine. Cover; let rise in warm place until double in volume, about 1-1/2 hours. Punch down dough; divide in half. Shape each half into twelve balls. Place 3 inches apart on greased cookie sheet; flatten to 3-inch circle. Cover; let rise until double in volume, about 45 minutes. Make depression in center of each roll; fill with Cream Cheese Filling. Bake at 375°, 8 to 10 minutes or until golden brown. Remove from cookie sheet; sprinkle with confectioners' sugar, if desired.

Cream Cheese Filling

1 **8-oz. pkg. Philadelphia Brand cream cheese**
¼ **cup sugar**

1 **egg**
¼ **teaspoon grated lemon rind**

Combine softened cream cheese and remaining ingredients, mixing until well blended.

2 dozen

Orange Tea Ring

2 cups flour
½ cup granulated sugar
2 teaspoons baking powder
½ teaspoon salt
½ cup Parkay margarine
½ cup milk
1 8-oz. pkg. Philadelphia Brand cream cheese
½ cup raisins

¼ cup chopped almonds
1 tablespoon grated orange rind

*   *   *

1½ cups sifted confectioners' sugar
2 tablespoons Kraft pasteurized orange juice

Combine flour, 1/4 cup granulated sugar, baking powder and salt; cut in margarine until mixture resembles coarse crumbs. Add milk, mixing just until moistened. On lightly floured surface, knead dough five times. Roll out dough to 18 × 12-inch rectangle; spread with softened cream cheese. Sprinkle with combined remaining granulated sugar, raisins, nuts and orange rind. Roll up from long end; seal long end. Shape into ring, seam-side down, on well greased cookie sheet; seal ends. Cut two-thirds through ring from outer edge at 1-inch intervals; turn each section on its side. Bake at 375°, 25 to 30 minutes or until lightly browned.

Combine confectioners' sugar and orange juice; mix well. Drizzle over warm tea ring.

Poppy Seed Bread

1 cup all-purpose biscuit mix
⅓ cup milk
2 medium onions, sliced
2 tablespoons Parkay margarine

1 8-oz. pkg. Philadelphia Brand cream cheese
1 egg
½ teaspoon salt
1 teaspoon poppy seeds

Combine biscuit mix and milk; mix well. Spread into greased 9-inch square baking pan or pie plate. Sauté onion in margarine. Combine softened cream cheese, egg and salt, mixing until well blended. Stir in onion. Spread cream cheese mixture over biscuit dough; sprinkle with poppy seeds. Bake at 450°, 20 minutes.

Apricot Crumble Cake

With a layer of preserves in the center and a bubbly coconut topping this coffee cake is a guaranteed favorite for friends or family.

1¼ cups granulated sugar
1 8-oz. pkg. Philadelphia Brand cream cheese
½ cup Parkay margarine
2 eggs
1 teaspoon vanilla
2 cups sifted cake flour
1 teaspoon baking powder
½ teaspoon baking soda
¼ teaspoon salt

¼ cup milk
1 10-oz. jar Kraft apricot or peach preserves
* * *
2 cups shredded coconut
⅔ cup packed brown sugar
⅓ cup Parkay margarine, melted
1 teaspoon cinnamon

Combine granulated sugar, softened cream cheese and margarine, mixing until well blended. Blend in eggs and vanilla. Sift together cake flour, baking powder, baking soda and salt. Add to cream cheese mixture alternately with milk, mixing well after each addition. Pour half of batter into greased and floured 13 × 9-inch baking pan. Dot with preserves; cover with remaining batter. Bake at 350°, 35 to 40 minutes or until wooden pick inserted in center comes out clean.

Combine coconut, brown sugar, margarine and cinnamon; mix well. Spread on cake; broil until golden brown.

Variations: Substitute 10-oz. jar pineapple, red raspberry or cherry preserves for apricot.
Substitute 1/2 cup chopped pecans or walnuts or 1/2 cup sliced almonds for 1 cup coconut.

Orange Nugget Coffee Cake

1¼ cups sugar
½ cup Parkay margarine
2 eggs
2¼ cups flour
1 tablespoon baking powder
1 teaspoon salt
¾ cup milk
¼ cup water

1 8-oz. pkg. Philadelphia Brand cream cheese, cubed
½ cup chopped nuts
1 tablespoon grated orange rind

*   *   *

¼ cup sugar
2 teaspoons grated orange rind

Cream sugar and margarine until light and fluffy. Blend in eggs. Add combined dry ingredients alternately with milk and water, mixing well after each addition. Fold in cream cheese, nuts and orange rind. Pour into greased and floured 13 × 9-inch baking pan.

Combine sugar and orange rind; sprinkle over batter. Bake at 375°, 35 to 40 minutes.

Variation: Substitute greased and floured 9 × 5-inch loaf pan for baking pan. Decrease topping to 2 tablespoons sugar and 1 teaspoon grated orange rind. Bake at 375°, 1 hour and 15 to 20 minutes.

Sweet Potato Cheesecake — page 108
Special Occasion Cheesecake — page 123
Centennial Cheesecake — page 109

ELEGANT CHEESECAKES

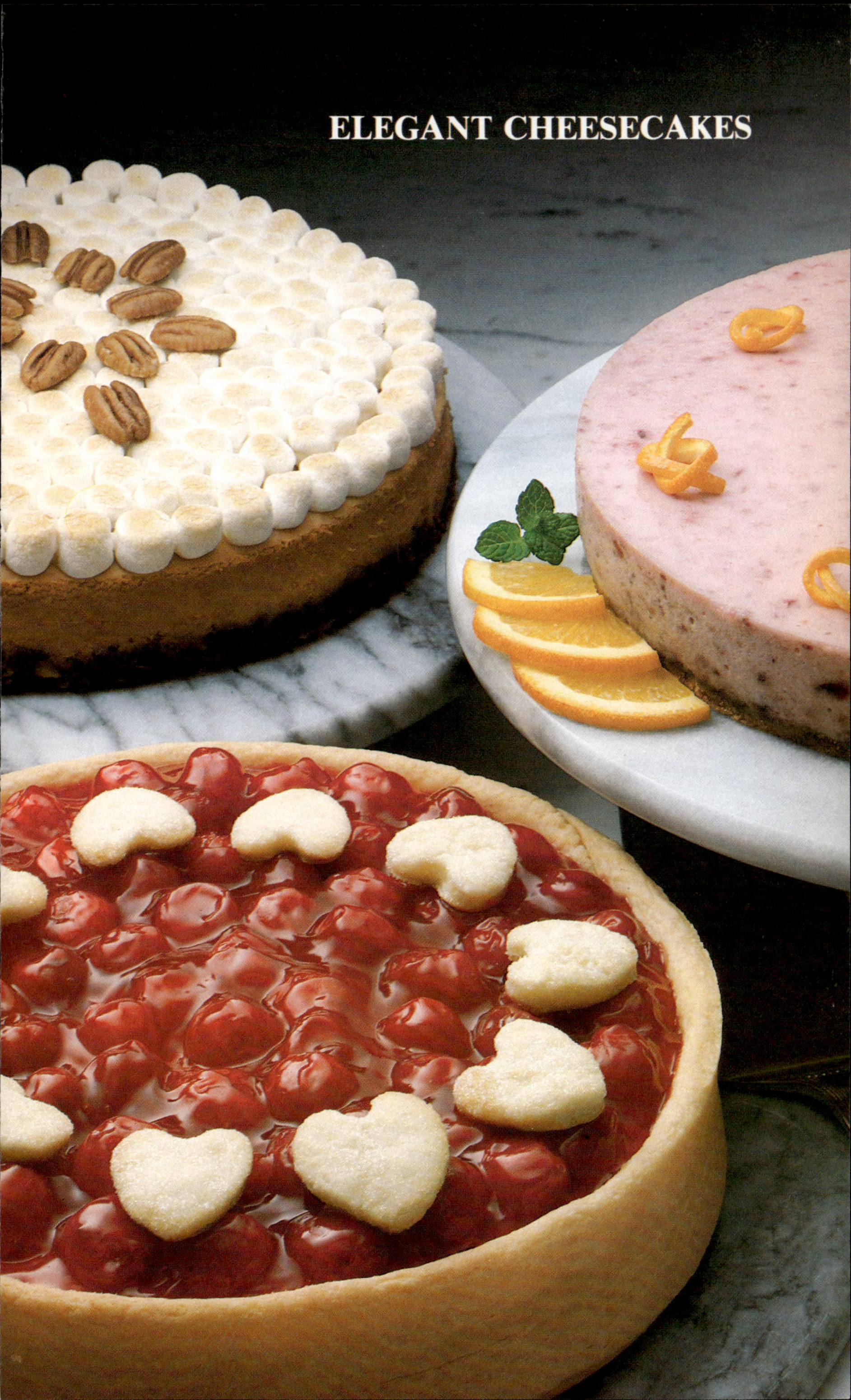

Sweet Potato Cheesecake

1 cup gingersnap crumbs
½ cup finely chopped pecans
3 tablespoons Parkay
   margarine, melted
    *   *   *
2 8-oz. pkgs. Philadelphia
   Brand cream cheese
1 17-oz. can sweet potatoes,
   drained

½ cup sugar
¼ cup Kraft pasteurized
   orange juice
2 eggs
½ cup dairy sour cream
1 teaspoon cinnamon
   Kraft miniature
   marshmallows

Combine crumbs, nuts and margarine; press onto bottom of 9-inch springform pan.

Combine softened cream cheese, sweet potatoes and sugar, mixing on electric mixer until well blended. Blend in orange juice, eggs, sour cream and cinnamon; pour over crust. Bake at 325°, 1 hour. Loosen cake from rim of pan. Cool; remove rim. Chill. Top with marshmallows just before serving; broil until lightly browned. Garnish with pecan halves, if desired.

Tom and Jerry Cheesecake

1 cup vanilla wafer crumbs
¼ cup Parkay margarine,
   melted
    *   *   *
4 cups Kraft miniature
   marshmallows

⅓ cup Kraft pasteurized
   orange juice
2 8-oz. pkgs. Philadelphia
   Brand cream cheese
1 teaspoon rum flavoring
1 cup whipping cream,
   whipped

Combine crumbs and margarine; press onto bottom of 9-inch springform pan. Bake at 325°, 10 minutes. Cool.

Melt marshmallows with orange juice over low heat; stir occasionally until smooth. Chill until slightly thickened; mix until well blended. Combine softened cream cheese and flavoring, mixing on electric mixer until well blended. Add marshmallow mixture; mix well. Fold in whipped cream; pour over crust. Chill. Garnish with maraschino cherries and pecan halves, if desired.

Centennial Cheesecake

A spectacular cheesecake in a cream cheese crust developed for a very special occasion — the 100th birthday of Phila-delphia Brand cream cheese.

1 8-oz. pkg. Philadelphia Brand cream cheese	1 cup sugar
½ cup Parkay margarine	2 tablespoons flour
1½ cups flour	1 tablespoon lemon juice
Sugar	2 teaspoons grated lemon rind
1 teaspoon grated lemon rind	4 eggs
* * *	1 21-oz. can cherry pie filling
3 8-oz. pkgs. Philadelphia Brand cream cheese	

Combine softened cream cheese and margarine, mixing until well blended. Add flour, 1/4 cup sugar and lemon rind; mix well. Form into ball; chill thoroughly. On lightly floured surface, roll 1/4 cup dough to 1/8-inch thickness. Cut with assorted 1-inch cutters. Sprinkle with sugar; place on ungreased cookie sheet. Bake at 375°, 8 to 10 minutes or until edges are very lightly browned. Spread two-thirds remaining dough onto bottom of 9-inch springform pan. Bake at 375°, 25 minutes. Cool. Press remaining dough around sides of pan.

Combine softened cream cheese, sugar, flour, lemon juice and rind, mixing on electric mixer until well blended. Blend in eggs; pour into crust. Bake at 300°, 1 hour and 15 minutes. Loosen cake from rim of pan. Cool; remove rim. Spoon pie filling over cheesecake; top with cut outs. Chill.

Variations: Substitute any of the following for pie filling:
- Mandarin orange segments and drained crushed pineapple
- Kraft raspberry preserves and peach slices
- Dairy sour cream and strawberry halves
- Kiwi fruit slices
- Shaved chocolate and nuts
- Pineapple slices and maraschino cherries
- Assorted fruits

Carrot 'n Raisin Cheesecake

Children will love it — a spicy orange cheesecake filled with shredded carrots and raisins.

1 cup graham cracker crumbs

3 tablespoons granulated sugar

½ teaspoon cinnamon

3 tablespoons Parkay margarine, melted

*   *   *

3 8-oz. pkgs. Philadelphia Brand cream cheese

½ cup granulated sugar

½ cup flour

4 eggs

¼ cup Kraft pasteurized orange juice

1 cup finely shredded carrots

¼ cup raisins

½ teaspoon nutmeg

¼ teaspoon ginger

*   *   *

2 tablespoons Kraft pasteurized orange juice

Dash of salt

2½ cups sifted confectioners' sugar

¼ cup raisins

Combine crumbs, granulated sugar, cinnamon and margarine; press onto bottom of 9-inch springform pan. Bake at 325°, 10 minutes.

Combine 2-1/2 packages softened cream cheese, granulated sugar and 1/4 cup flour, mixing on electric mixer until well blended. Blend in eggs and orange juice. Add combined remaining flour, carrots, raisins and spices; mix well. Pour over crust. Bake at 450°, 10 minutes. Reduce oven temperature to 250°; continue baking 55 minutes. Loosen cake from rim of pan. Cool; remove rim.

Combine remaining softened cream cheese, orange juice and salt, mixing until well blended. Gradually add confectioners' sugar, mixing well after each addition. Pour over cheesecake. Garnish with raisins.

Harvest Pumpkin Cheesecake

A great alternative to traditional pumpkin pie — a spicy pumpkin cheesecake in a gingersnap crust.

1 cup gingersnap crumbs
½ cup finely chopped pecans
3 tablespoons Parkay margarine, melted
      *   *   *
1 8-oz. pkg. Philadelphia Brand cream cheese
¼ cup sugar
½ teaspoon vanilla
1 egg
      *   *   *

1 16-oz. can pumpkin
⅔ cup (5⅓-fl. oz. can) evaporated milk
½ cup sugar
2 eggs
1 teaspoon cinnamon
¼ teaspoon ginger
¼ teaspoon nutmeg
Dash of salt

Combine crumbs, nuts and margarine; press onto bottom of 9-inch springform pan.

Combine softened cream cheese, sugar and vanilla, mixing on electric mixer until well blended. Blend in egg; pour over crust.

Combine remaining ingredients; mix well. Carefully pour over cream cheese mixture. Bake at 325°, 1 hour and 30 to 35 minutes or until set. Loosen cake from rim of pan. Cool; remove rim. Chill.

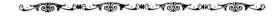

Creamy Cocoa Cheesecake

1 cup graham cracker
  crumbs
3 tablespoons sugar
3 tablespoons Parkay
  margarine, melted
    *   *   *
2 8-oz. pkgs. Philadelphia
  Brand cream cheese

¾ cup sugar
⅓ cup cocoa
1 teaspoon vanilla
2 eggs
    *   *   *
1 cup dairy sour cream
2 tablespoons sugar
1 teaspoon vanilla

Combine crumbs, sugar and margarine; press onto bottom and sides of 9-inch springform pan.

Combine softened cream cheese, sugar, cocoa and vanilla, mixing on electric mixer until well blended. Blend in eggs; pour into crust. Bake at 375°, 30 minutes.

Combine sour cream, sugar and vanilla; carefully spread over cheesecake. Bake at 425°, 10 minutes. Loosen cake from rim of pan. Cool; remove rim. Chill.

Washington Cheesecake

1 cup graham cracker
  crumbs
3 tablespoons sugar
3 tablespoons Parkay
  margarine, melted
    *   *   *
3 8-oz. pkgs. Philadelphia
  Brand cream cheese

¾ cup sugar
2 tablespoons flour
3 eggs
2 tablespoons milk
1 teaspoon vanilla
1 21-oz. can cherry pie
  filling

Combine crumbs, sugar and margarine; press onto bottom of 9-inch springform pan. Bake at 325°, 10 minutes.

Combine softened cream cheese, sugar and flour, mixing on electric mixer until well blended. Blend in eggs, milk and vanilla; pour over crust. Bake at 450°, 10 minutes. Reduce oven temperature to 250°; continue baking 25 to 30 minutes or until set. Loosen cake from rim of pan. Cool; remove rim. Chill. Top with pie filling before serving.

Lattice Cherry Cheesecake

1 18-oz. roll refrigerated
   sugar slice-and-bake
   cookies
   *   *   *
2 8-oz. pkgs. Philadelphia
   Brand cream cheese

1 cup dairy sour cream
¾ cup sugar
¼ teaspoon almond extract
3 eggs
1 21-oz. can cherry pie
   filling

Cut cookie dough into 1/8-inch slices. Arrange cookie slices, slightly overlapping, onto bottom and sides of greased 9-inch springform pan; press edges to form crust.

Combine softened cream cheese, sour cream, sugar and extract, mixing on electric mixer until well blended. Blend in eggs. Reserve 1/4 cup mixture; pour remaining mixture into crust. Bake at 350°, 1 hour and 10 minutes. Increase oven temperature to 450°. Spoon pie filling over cheesecake; top with reserved cream cheese mixture, creating a lattice design. Bake at 450°, 10 minutes. Loosen cake from rim of pan. Cool; remove rim. Chill.

Marble Cheesecake

1 cup graham cracker
   crumbs
3 tablespoons sugar
3 tablespoons Parkay
   margarine, melted
   *   *   *
3 8-oz. pkgs. Philadelphia
   Brand cream cheese

¾ cup sugar
3 tablespoons flour
1 teaspoon vanilla
3 eggs
1 1-oz. square unsweetened
   chocolate, melted

Combine crumbs, sugar and margarine; press onto bottom of 9-inch springform pan. Bake at 350°, 10 minutes.

Combine softened cream cheese, sugar, flour and vanilla, mixing on electric mixer until well blended. Blend in eggs. Blend chocolate into 1 cup batter. Spoon plain and chocolate batters alternately over crust; cut through batter with knife several times for marble effect. Bake at 450°, 10 minutes. Reduce oven temperature to 250°; continue baking 30 minutes. Loosen cake from rim of pan. Cool; remove rim. Chill.

Hollywood Cheesecake

A famous favorite and a star among cheesecakes — a Kraft Kitchens original.

1 cup graham cracker
   crumbs
3 tablespoons sugar
3 tablespoons Parkay
   margarine, melted
   *   *   *

2 8-oz. pkgs. Philadelphia
   Brand cream cheese
½ cup sugar

1 tablespoon lemon juice
1 teaspoon grated lemon
   rind
½ teaspoon vanilla
2 eggs, separated
   *   *   *

1 cup dairy sour cream
2 tablespoons sugar
1 teaspoon vanilla

Combine crumbs, sugar and margarine; press onto bottom of 9-inch springform pan. Bake at 325°, 10 minutes.

Combine softened cream cheese, sugar, lemon juice, rind and vanilla, mixing on electric mixer until well blended. Blend in egg yolks. Fold in stiffly beaten egg whites; pour over crust. Bake at 300°, 45 minutes.

Combine sour cream, sugar and vanilla; carefully spread over cheesecake. Continue baking 10 minutes. Loosen cake from rim of pan. Cool; remove rim. Chill.

Metropolitan Cheesecake

⅓ cup Parkay margarine
⅓ cup sugar
1 egg
1¼ cups flour
      *   *   *
3 8-oz. pkgs. Philadelphia
   Brand cream cheese
¾ cup sugar
1 tablespoon lemon juice

1 teaspoon grated lemon
   rind
3 eggs
      *   *   *
1 cup dairy sour cream
2 tablespoons sugar
1 teaspoon vanilla
1 21-oz. can cherry pie
   filling

Cream margarine and sugar until light and fluffy. Blend in egg. Add flour; mix well. Spread dough onto bottom and 1-1/2-inches high around sides of 9-inch springform pan. Bake at 450°, 5 minutes.

Combine softened cream cheese, sugar, lemon juice and rind, mixing on electric mixer until well blended. Blend in eggs; pour into crust. Bake at 450°, 10 minutes. Reduce oven temperature to 300°; continue baking 30 minutes.

Combine sour cream, sugar and vanilla; carefully spread over cheesecake. Continue baking 10 minutes. Loosen cake from rim of pan. Cool; remove rim. Chill. Top with pie filling before serving.

Variations: Substitute your favorite canned fruit pie filling for cherry.
Omit pie filling; top with fresh raspberries or sliced strawberries.

Cocoa-Nut Meringue Cheesecake

A fluffy marshmallow meringue atop a creamy cocoa cheesecake in a toasted coconut crust — magnificent!

1 7-oz. pkg. flaked coconut, toasted
¼ cup chopped pecans
3 tablespoons Parkay margarine, melted
* * *
2 8-oz. pkgs. Philadelphia Brand cream cheese
⅓ cup sugar

3 tablespoons cocoa
2 tablespoons water
1 teaspoon vanilla
3 eggs, separated
* * *
Dash of salt
1 7-oz. jar Kraft marshmallow creme
½ cup chopped pecans

Combine coconut, nuts and margarine; press onto bottom of 9-inch springform pan.

Combine softened cream cheese, sugar, cocoa, water and vanilla, mixing on electric mixer until well blended. Blend in egg yolks; pour over crust. Bake at 350°, 30 minutes. Loosen cake from rim of pan. Cool; remove rim.

Beat egg whites and salt until soft peaks form. Gradually add marshmallow creme, beating until stiff peaks form. Sprinkle nuts on cheesecake to within 1/2 inch of edge. Carefully spread marshmallow creme mixture over top of cheesecake to seal. Bake at 350°, 15 minutes. Cool.

Cocoa-Nut Meringue Cheesecake

Praline Cheesecake

1 cup graham cracker crumbs

3 tablespoons granulated sugar

3 tablespoons Parkay margarine, melted

    *   *   *

3 8-oz. pkgs. Philadelphia Brand cream cheese

1¼ cups packed dark brown sugar

2 tablespoons flour

3 eggs

1½ teaspoons vanilla

½ cup finely chopped pecans

Combine crumbs, granulated sugar and margarine; press onto bottom of 9-inch springform pan. Bake at 350°, 10 minutes.

Combine softened cream cheese, brown sugar and flour, mixing on electric mixer until well blended. Blend in eggs and vanilla; stir in nuts. Pour over crust. Bake at 450°, 10 minutes. Reduce oven temperature to 250°; continue baking 30 minutes. Loosen cake from rim of pan. Cool; remove rim. Chill. Brush with maple syrup and garnish with pecan halves, if desired.

Peanut Butter and Jelly Cheesecake

1 cup graham cracker crumbs

3 tablespoons sugar

3 tablespoons Parkay margarine, melted

    *   *   *

2 8-oz. pkgs. Philadelphia Brand cream cheese

1 cup sugar

½ cup chunk style peanut butter

½ cup milk

3 tablespoons flour

4 eggs

½ cup Kraft grape jelly

Combine crumbs, sugar and margarine; press onto bottom of 9-inch springform pan. Bake at 325°, 10 minutes.

Combine softened cream cheese, sugar, peanut butter, milk and flour, mixing on electric mixer until well blended. Blend in eggs; pour over crust. Bake at 450°, 10 minutes. Reduce oven temperature to 250°; continue baking 40 minutes. Loosen cake from rim of pan. Cool; remove rim. Heat jelly until melted; spoon over cheesecake. Chill.

Orange-Butterscotch Cheesecake

1¼ cups old fashioned or
    quick oats, uncooked
¼ cup packed brown sugar
2 tablespoons flour
⅓ cup Squeeze Parkay
    margarine
      *   *   *
3 8-oz. pkgs. Philadelphia
    Brand cream cheese
¾ cup granulated sugar

1 teaspoon grated orange
    rind
1 teaspoon vanilla
4 eggs
     *   *   *
½ cup packed brown sugar
⅓ cup light corn syrup
¼ cup Squeeze Parkay
    margarine
1 teaspoon vanilla

Combine oats, brown sugar, flour and margarine; press on-to bottom of 9-inch springform pan. Bake at 350°, 15 minutes.

Combine softened cream cheese, granulated sugar, orange rind and vanilla, mixing on electric mixer until well blended. Blend in eggs; pour over crust. Bake at 325°, 1 hour and 5 minutes. Loosen cake from rim of pan. Cool; remove rim.

Combine brown sugar, corn syrup and margarine; bring to boil, stirring constantly. Remove from heat; stir in vanilla. Chill until slightly thickened. Carefully spoon over cheese-cake. Chill. Garnish with orange slices, if desired.

Sun-Sational Cheesecake

This lovely, lemon sauced specialty is one of the most requested recipes from our television collection.

1 cup graham cracker crumbs	2 tablespoons lemon juice
3 tablespoons sugar	1 tablespoon grated lemon rind
3 tablespoons Parkay margarine, melted	½ teaspoon vanilla
* * *	4 eggs (1 separated)
3 8-oz. pkgs. Philadelphia Brand cream cheese	* * *
1 cup sugar	¾ cup sugar
3 tablespoons flour	2 tablespoons cornstarch
	½ cup water
	¼ cup lemon juice

Combine crumbs, sugar and margarine; press onto bottom of 9-inch springform pan. Bake at 325°, 10 minutes.

Combine softened cream cheese, sugar, flour, lemon juice, rind and vanilla, mixing on electric mixer until well blended. Blend in 3 eggs and 1 egg white; reserve yolk. Pour over crust. Bake at 450°, 10 minutes. Reduce oven temperature to 250°; continue baking 30 minutes. Loosen cake from rim of pan. Cool; remove rim.

In saucepan, combine sugar and cornstarch; gradually add water and lemon juice. Cook, stirring constantly, until clear and thickened. Stir small amount of hot mixture into reserved egg yolk; return to hot mixture. Cook 1 minute, stirring constantly. Spoon over cheesecake; chill. Garnish with lemon slices, if desired.

Supreme Cheesecake

1 cup graham cracker crumbs
3 tablespoons sugar
3 tablespoons Parkay margarine, melted

*   *   *

2 8-oz. pkgs. Philadelphia Brand cream cheese

½ cup sugar
2 tablespoons flour
½ teaspoon salt
4 eggs, separated
⅔ cup half and half
1 teaspoon vanilla

Combine crumbs, sugar and margarine; press onto bottom of 9-inch springform pan. Bake at 325°, 10 minutes.

Combine softened cream cheese, sugar, flour and salt, mixing on electric mixer until well blended. Blend in egg yolks, half and half and vanilla. Fold in stiffly beaten egg whites; pour over crust. Bake at 325°, 1 hour. Loosen cake from rim of pan. Cool; remove rim. Chill.

Tropical Cheesecake

1 cup shredded coconut
2 tablespoons flour
2 tablespoons Parkay margarine, melted

*   *   *

1 envelope unflavored gelatin
1 cup cold water
¾ cup sugar

3 eggs, separated
2 8-oz. pkgs. Philadelphia Brand cream cheese
¼ cup lime juice
1 teaspoon grated lime rind
Few drops green food coloring (optional)
1 cup whipping cream, whipped

Combine coconut, flour and margarine; press onto bottom of 9-inch springform pan. Bake at 350°, 15 minutes. Cool.

Soften gelatin in 1/4 cup cold water. In saucepan, combine remaining water, sugar and egg yolks; cook over medium heat 5 minutes, stirring constantly. Add gelatin; stir until dissolved. Gradually add to softened cream cheese, mixing on electric mixer until well blended. Blend in lime juice, rind and food coloring. Fold in stiffly beaten egg whites and whipped cream. Pour over crust; chill until firm.

Strawberry Glacé Cheesecake

Strictly for festive occasions — a high and creamy cheese-cake in a delicate pastry crust, gloriously glazed with straw-berries and Kirsch.

⅓ cup Parkay margarine	3 eggs
⅓ cup sugar	2 tablespoons milk
1 egg	1 teaspoon vanilla
1¼ cups flour	* * *
* * *	1 10-oz. jar Kraft strawberry
3 8-oz. pkgs. Philadelphia	jelly
Brand cream cheese	1 tablespoon Kirsch
¾ cup sugar	1 qt. whole strawberries
2 tablespoons flour	

Cream margarine and sugar until light and fluffy. Blend in egg. Add flour; mix well. Spread dough onto bottom and 1-1/2-inches high around sides of 9-inch springform pan. Bake at 450°, 5 minutes.

Combine softened cream cheese, sugar and flour, mixing on electric mixer until well blended. Blend in eggs, milk and vanilla; pour into crust. Bake at 450°, 10 minutes. Reduce oven temperature to 250°; continue baking 30 minutes. Loosen cake from rim of pan. Cool; remove rim. Chill.

Heat jelly until melted. Cool slightly; stir in Kirsch. Arrange strawberries on top of cheesecake; spoon jelly mixture over strawberries. Chill.

Special Occasion Cheesecake

1 cup graham cracker crumbs
3 tablespoons sugar
3 tablespoons Parkay margarine, melted
 * * *
1 envelope unflavored gelatin
½ cup cranberry juice

2 8-oz. containers soft Philadelphia Brand cream cheese
1 7-oz. jar Kraft marshmallow creme
1 10-oz. pkg. frozen cranberry-orange relish, thawed

Combine crumbs, sugar and margarine; press onto bottom of 9-inch springform pan. Bake at 325°, 10 minutes. Cool.

Soften gelatin in cranberry juice; stir over low heat until dissolved. Gradually add to cream cheese, mixing on electric mixer until well blended. Blend in marshmallow creme; fold in relish. Pour over crust; chill until firm. Garnish with orange twists, if desired.

Rocky Road Cheesecake

1 cup chocolate wafer crumbs
3 tablespoons Parkay margarine, melted
 * * *
1 envelope unflavored gelatin
¼ cup cold water
2 8-oz. containers soft Philadelphia Brand cream cheese

¾ cup sugar
⅓ cup cocoa
½ teaspoon vanilla
Dash of salt
2 cups Kraft miniature marshmallows
1 cup whipping cream, whipped
½ cup chopped nuts

Combine crumbs and margarine; press onto bottom of 9-inch springform pan. Bake at 350°, 10 minutes. Cool.

Soften gelatin in cold water; stir over low heat until dissolved. Combine cream cheese, sugar, cocoa, vanilla and salt, mixing on electric mixer until well blended. Gradually add gelatin, mixing until blended. Fold in remaining ingredients. Pour over crust; chill until firm.

Peppermint Cheesecake

The family favorite — a cool and creamy cheesecake made with easy-to-blend soft cream cheese and flavored with peppermint candy and milk chocolate.

1 cup chocolate wafer crumbs

3 tablespoons Parkay margarine, melted

*   *   *

1 envelope unflavored gelatin

¼ cup cold water

2 8-oz. containers soft Philadelphia Brand cream cheese

½ cup sugar

½ cup milk

¼ cup crushed peppermint candy

1 cup whipping cream, whipped

2 1.05-oz. milk chocolate candy bars, finely chopped

Combine crumbs and margarine; press onto bottom of 9-inch springform pan. Bake at 350°, 10 minutes. Cool.

Soften gelatin in cold water; stir over low heat until dissolved. Combine cream cheese and sugar, mixing on electric mixer until well blended. Gradually add gelatin, milk and peppermint candy, mixing until blended; chill until slightly thickened. Fold in whipped cream and chocolate. Pour over crust; chill until firm. Garnish with additional whipped cream and crushed peppermint candy, if desired.

Peppermint Cheesecake

Key Lime Cheesecake

1½ cups chocolate wafer crumbs	3 eggs, separated
2 tablespoons sugar	½ cup sugar
⅓ cup Parkay margarine, melted	1 teaspoon grated lime rind
* * *	2 8-oz. containers soft Philadelphia Brand cream cheese
1 envelope unflavored gelatin	Few drops green food coloring (optional)
¼ cup lime juice	

Combine crumbs, sugar and margarine; press onto bottom of 9-inch springform pan. Bake at 325°, 10 minutes. Cool.

Soften gelatin in lime juice; stir over low heat until dissolved. Add combined egg yolks, 1/4 cup sugar and lime rind; cook over low heat 5 minutes, stirring constantly. Cool. Gradually add to cream cheese, mixing on electric mixer until well blended. Add food coloring. Beat egg whites until foamy; gradually add remaining sugar, beating until stiff peaks form. Fold into cream cheese mixture. Pour over crust; chill until firm.

Creamy Orange Cheesecake

1 cup graham cracker crumbs	¼ cup cold water
3 tablespoons sugar	2 8-oz. containers soft Philadelphia Brand cream cheese
3 tablespoons Parkay margarine, melted	
* * *	¾ cup Kraft pasteurized orange juice
1 envelope unflavored gelatin	1 7-oz. jar Kraft marshmallow creme

Combine crumbs, sugar and margarine; press onto bottom of 9-inch springform pan. Bake at 325°, 10 minutes. Cool.

Soften gelatin in cold water; stir over low heat until dissolved. Gradually add to cream cheese, mixing on electric mixer until well blended. Blend in orange juice and marshmallow creme; chill until slightly thickened. Pour over crust; chill until firm. Garnish with whipped cream, if desired.

Berry Cool Cheesecake

1 **cup graham cracker crumbs**
3 **tablespoons sugar**
3 **tablespoons Parkay margarine, melted**
* * *
1 **envelope unflavored gelatin**
¼ **cup cold water**

1 **10-oz. pkg. frozen strawberries, thawed**
Milk
2 **8-oz. containers soft Philadelphia Brand cream cheese**
1 **7-oz. jar Kraft marshmallow creme**
Dash of salt

Combine crumbs, sugar and margarine; press onto bottom of 9-inch springform pan. Bake at 350°, 10 minutes. Cool.

Soften gelatin in cold water; stir over low heat until dissolved. Drain strawberries, reserving syrup. Add enough milk to syrup to measure 1 cup. Gradually add combined syrup mixture and gelatin to cream cheese, mixing on electric mixer until well blended. Blend in marshmallow creme and salt; fold in strawberries. Pour over crust; chill until firm.

Creamy Cool Cheesecake

1 **cup graham cracker crumbs**
¼ **cup sugar**
¼ **cup Parkay margarine, melted**
* * *
1 **envelope unflavored gelatin**
¼ **cup cold water**

2 **8-oz. containers soft Philadelphia Brand cream cheese**
½ **cup sugar**
Dash of salt
½ **cup milk**
1 **cup whipping cream, whipped**
Peaches, strawberries or blueberries

Combine crumbs, sugar and margarine; press onto bottom of 9-inch springform pan.

Soften gelatin in cold water; stir over low heat until dissolved. Combine cream cheese, sugar and salt, mixing on electric mixer until well blended. Gradually add gelatin and milk, mixing until blended; chill until slightly thickened. Fold in whipped cream. Pour over crust; chill until firm. Top with fruit.

Lemon Delight Cheesecake

1½ cups graham cracker
   crumbs
¼ cup sugar
½ cup Parkay margarine,
   melted
      *   *   *
1 envelope unflavored
   gelatin
⅓ cup cold water

3 eggs, separated
½ cup sugar
2 8-oz. containers soft
   Philadelphia Brand
   cream cheese
⅓ cup lemon juice
1 teaspoon grated lemon
   rind

Combine crumbs, sugar and margarine; reserve 1/2 cup. Press remaining crumb mixture onto bottom of 9-inch springform pan.

Soften gelatin in cold water. In saucepan, combine egg yolks and 1/4 cup sugar; cook over low heat 5 minutes, stirring constantly. Add gelatin; stir until dissolved. Gradually add to cream cheese, mixing on electric mixer until well blended. Blend in lemon juice and rind. Beat egg whites until foamy; gradually add remaining sugar, beating until stiff peaks form. Fold into cream cheese mixture, pour over crust. Top with reserved crumbs; chill until firm.

Creme de Menthe Pie — page 130
Pineapple ''Philly'' Pie — page 131
Paradise Pumpkin Pie — page 130

Creme de Menthe Pie

2 cups (24) crushed chocolate cream-filled cookies

¼ cup Parkay margarine, melted

*   *   *

2 8-oz. pkgs. Philadelphia Brand cream cheese

1½ cups sifted confectioners' sugar

2 tablespoons creme de menthe

2 cups whipping cream

Combine crumbs and margarine; press onto bottom and sides of 9-inch pie plate.

Combine softened cream cheese, 1/4 cup sugar and creme de menthe, mixing until well blended. Gradually add remaining sugar to cream, beating until stiff peaks form. Fold into cream cheese mixture. Pour into crust; chill several hours or overnight. Garnish with shaved chocolate, if desired.

Paradise Pumpkin Pie

1 8-oz. pkg. Philadelphia Brand cream cheese

¼ cup sugar

½ teaspoon vanilla

1 egg

1 9-inch unbaked pastry shell

*   *   *

1¼ cups canned pumpkin

1 cup evaporated milk

½ cup sugar

2 eggs, slightly beaten

1 teaspoon cinnamon

¼ teaspoon ginger

¼ teaspoon nutmeg

Dash of salt

Combine softened cream cheese, sugar and vanilla, mixing until well blended. Blend in egg. Spread onto bottom of pastry shell.

Combine remaining ingredients; mix well. Carefully pour over cream cheese mixture. Bake at 350°, 1 hour and 5 minutes. Cool. Brush with maple syrup and garnish with pecan halves, if desired.

Pineapple "Philly" Pie

A memorable pineapple pie with a cream cheese custard topping — a popular Kraft pie since the early '50s.

⅓ cup sugar
1 tablespoon cornstarch
1 8¼-oz. can crushed pineapple, undrained
1 9-inch unbaked pastry shell

     *   *   *

1 8-oz. pkg. Philadelphia Brand cream cheese

½ cup sugar
½ teaspoon salt
½ cup milk
2 eggs
½ teaspoon vanilla
¼ cup chopped pecans

In saucepan, combine sugar and cornstarch; gradually add pineapple. Cook, stirring constantly, until clear and thickened. Cool; spread onto bottom of pastry shell.

Combine softened cream cheese, sugar and salt, mixing until well blended. Blend in milk, eggs and vanilla. Pour over pineapple mixture; sprinkle with nuts. Bake at 400°, 15 minutes. Reduce oven temperature to 325°; continue baking 40 minutes. Garnish with pineapple slices, cut in half, and maraschino cherry halves, if desired.

Regal Strawberry Pie

"Regal" is right! — a "cheesecake" pie glazed with strawberry preserves and topped with whipped cream.

1 8-oz. pkg. Philadelphia Brand cream cheese
½ cup sugar
½ cup milk
3 eggs

1 teaspoon vanilla
1 9-inch baked pastry shell
1 10-oz. jar Kraft strawberry preserves

Combine softened cream cheese and sugar, mixing until well blended. Blend in milk, eggs and vanilla. Pour into pastry shell. Bake at 350°, 40 minutes. Cool. Top with preserves; chill. Garnish with whipped cream, if desired.

Chocolate Cloud Pie

A double chocolate delight — a chocolate cream cheese filling in a crispy chocolate crumb crust.

1¼ cups chocolate wafer crumbs

2 tablespoons granulated sugar

¼ cup Parkay margarine, melted

* * *

2 8-oz. pkgs. Philadelphia Brand cream cheese

¾ cup packed brown sugar

1 teaspoon vanilla

1 6-oz. pkg. semi-sweet chocolate pieces, melted

2 eggs

Combine crumbs, granulated sugar and margarine; press onto bottom and sides of 9-inch pie plate. Bake at 325°, 10 minutes. Cool.

Combine softened cream cheese, brown sugar and vanilla, mixing until well blended. Blend in chocolate and eggs. Pour into crust. Bake at 325°, 35 minutes. Chill.

Cream Cheese Pastry

This tender, flaky pastry is a famous Kraft Kitchens' specialty.

1 8-oz. pkg. Philadelphia Brand cream cheese

1 cup Parkay margarine

2 cups flour

½ teaspoon salt

Combine softened cream cheese and margarine, mixing until well blended. Add flour and salt; mix well. Form into ball; chill. Divide dough in half. On lightly floured surface, roll out each half to 12-inch circle. Place in two 9-inch pie plates. Trim and flute edges; prick bottom and sides with fork. Bake at 450°, 12 to 15 minutes or until golden brown.

Two 9-inch pastry shells

Variation: For tart shells, divide dough into twenty-four balls. Roll out each to 6-inch circle. Place in 4-inch tart pans. Trim and flute edges; prick with fork. Bake at 450°, 8 to 10 minutes or until golden brown.

"Philly" Cranberry Pie

1 8-oz. pkg. Philadelphia
  Brand cream cheese
2 tablespoons sugar
1 9-inch baked pastry shell
    *   *   *

1½ cups cranberries
⅔ cup Kraft pasteurized
  orange juice

¾ cup sugar
1 envelope unflavored
  gelatin
1 cup chopped orange
  sections
½ cup chopped nuts

Combine softened cream cheese and sugar, mixing until well blended. Spread onto bottom of pastry shell.

Combine cranberries and 1/3 cup orange juice; heat until skins pop. Add sugar; continue cooking 5 minutes. Soften gelatin in remaining orange juice; stir over low heat until dissolved. Gradually add gelatin to cranberry mixture, mixing until blended. Add orange sections and nuts; mix lightly. Cool. Spoon over cream cheese mixture; chill until firm. Garnish with additional orange sections, if desired.

Apple Glacé Pie

1 8-oz. pkg. Philadelphia
  Brand cream cheese
2 tablespoons sugar
1 tablespoon milk
1 teaspoon vanilla
1 9-inch baked pastry shell
    *   *   *

⅔ cup water
½ cup sugar
¼ cup red cinnamon candies
4 cups peeled apple slices
1 tablespoon lemon juice
2 teaspoons cornstarch

Combine softened cream cheese, sugar, milk and vanilla, mixing until well blended. Spread mixture onto bottom of pastry shell.

Heat water, sugar and candy over low heat; stir until candy is melted. Add apples; continue cooking 8 to 10 minutes or until apples are tender. Drain, reserving 1/2 cup liquid. In saucepan, combine reserved liquid, lemon juice and cornstarch; cook, stirring constantly, until clear and thickened. Arrange apples over cream cheese mixture; cover with glaze. Chill.

Blueberry Cream Pie

1 cup vanilla wafer crumbs
½ cup finely chopped pecans
⅓ cup Parkay margarine, melted
* * *
1 21-oz. can blueberry pie filling

1 teaspoon lemon juice
1 8-oz. pkg. Philadelphia Brand cream cheese
½ cup sifted confectioners' sugar
1 tablespoon milk
1 cup whipping cream

Combine crumbs, nuts and margarine; press onto bottom and sides of 9-inch pie plate. Bake at 350°, 10 minutes. Cool.

Combine pie filling and lemon juice; pour into crust. Combine softened cream cheese, 1/4 cup sugar and milk, mixing until well blended. Gradually add remaining sugar to cream, beating until stiff peaks form. Fold into cream cheese mixture. Pour over pie filling; chill several hours or overnight.

Variation: Substitute cherry or apple pie filling for blueberry pie filling.

Sunburst Peach Pie

2 8-oz. pkgs. Philadelphia Brand cream cheese
¼ cup sugar
2 tablespoons milk
½ teaspoon vanilla
1 9-inch baked pastry shell
1 16-oz. pkg. frozen peach slices, thawed, drained
* * *

2 tablespoons sugar
1 tablespoon cornstarch
½ cup water
1 tablespoon lemon juice
¼ cup Kraft red raspberry preserves

Combine softened cream cheese, sugar, milk and vanilla, mixing until well blended. Pour into pastry shell; top with peaches.

In saucepan, combine sugar and cornstarch; gradually add water and lemon juice. Cook, stirring constantly, until clear and thickened. Stir in preserves; cool slightly. Spoon over peaches; chill.

Blueberry Cream Pie

Bewitching Blueberry Pie

A cheesecake pie with a marvelous blueberry topping — a fancy pie for family occasions.

1   8-oz. pkg. Philadelphia
     Brand cream cheese
½   cup sugar
½   teaspoon salt
½   cup milk
2   eggs
½   teaspoon vanilla

1   9-inch unbaked pastry
     shell
     *   *   *
2   tablespoons sugar
1   tablespoon cornstarch
1   cup water
2   cups blueberries

Combine softened cream cheese, sugar and salt, mixing until well blended. Blend in milk, eggs and vanilla. Pour into pastry shell. Bake at 400°, 15 minutes. Reduce oven temperature to 325°; continue baking 20 minutes.

In saucepan, combine sugar and cornstarch; gradually add water. Cook, stirring constantly, until clear and thickened. Add berries; continue cooking 5 minutes. Cool slightly; spoon over cream cheese mixture. Chill.

Sunny Banana Pie

Treat the kids to this banana cream pie, made easy with a commercial crumb crust, cream cheese and pudding mix.

2   bananas
1   9-inch graham cracker
     crust
2   cups milk

1   8-oz. pkg. Philadelphia
     Brand cream cheese
1   3¼-oz. pkg. instant vanilla
     pudding mix

Slice bananas into crust. Gradually add 1/2 cup milk to softened cream cheese, mixing until well blended. Add remaining milk and pudding mix; beat slowly 1 minute. Pour into crust; chill. Garnish with toasted coconut, if desired.

Variation: Substitute 1-1/2 cups fresh peach slices for bananas.

Crunchy Crust Peanut Pie

A creamy peanut butter filling in a peanut crumb crust —
delicious.

1 **cup graham cracker crumbs**	1 **8-oz. pkg. Philadelphia Brand cream cheese**
¼ **cup chopped peanuts**	½ **cup sugar**
¼ **cup sugar**	¼ **cup peanut butter**
¼ **cup Parkay margarine, melted**	1 **tablespoon milk**
* * *	1 **cup whipping cream, whipped**

Combine crumbs, nuts, sugar and margarine; press onto bottom and sides of 9-inch pie plate.

Combine softened cream cheese, sugar, peanut butter and milk, mixing until well blended. Fold in whipped cream. Pour into crust; chill several hours or overnight. Garnish with additional chopped peanuts, if desired.

Sunrise Cherry Pie

1 **8¼-oz. can crushed pineapple, undrained**	¼ **cup sifted confectioners' sugar**
1 **8-oz. pkg. Philadelphia Brand cream cheese**	1 **cup whipping cream**
½ **teaspoon vanilla**	1 **9-inch graham cracker crust**
1 **21-oz. can cherry pie filling**	

Drain pineapple, reserving two tablespoons syrup. Combine reserved syrup, softened cream cheese and vanilla, mixing until well blended. Add 1/4 cup pineapple and 1/2 cup pie filling; mix lightly. Gradually add sugar to cream, beating until stiff peaks form. Fold into cream cheese mixture. Pour into crust; top with remaining pineapple and pie filling. Chill several hours or overnight.

Tropical Apricot Pie

1½ cups graham cracker
    crumbs
¼ cup sugar
⅓ cup Parkay margarine,
    melted

    *   *   *

1 8-oz. pkg. Philadelphia
    Brand cream cheese
⅓ cup sugar

½ teaspoon rum flavoring
1 envelope unflavored
    gelatin
½ cup cold water
1 20-oz. can apricot halves,
    drained
1 cup whipping cream,
    whipped
½ cup flaked coconut

Combine crumbs, sugar and margarine; press onto bottom and sides of 9-inch pie plate. Bake at 325°, 10 minutes. Cool.

Combine softened cream cheese, sugar and flavoring, mixing until well blended. Soften gelatin in cold water; stir over low heat until dissolved. Gradually add to cream cheese mixture, mixing until well blended. Chill until partially set. Reserve 1/2 cup apricot halves; chop remaining apricots. Fold chopped apricots, whipped cream and coconut into cream cheese mixture. Pour into crust; chill until firm. Top with reserved apricot halves.

Carameled Pecan Pie

This cream cheese custard pie has a hidden layer of crunchy pecans and caramel topping.

1 cup pecan halves
1 9-inch unbaked pastry
    shell
¼ cup Kraft caramel topping

2 8-oz. pkgs. Philadelphia
    Brand cream cheese
½ cup sugar
1 teaspoon vanilla
3 eggs

Place nuts in bottom of pastry shell; cover with topping. Combine softened cream cheese, sugar and vanilla, mixing until well blended. Blend in eggs. Pour over topping. Bake at 325°, 45 minutes. Chill. Garnish with additional nuts and drizzle with additional topping, if desired.

German Chocolate Pie

1½ cups coconut, toasted
½ cup chopped pecans
2 tablespoons flour
¼ cup Parkay margarine, melted

     *   *   *

2 8-oz. pkgs. Philadelphia Brand cream cheese
½ cup sugar
2 1-oz. squares sweet chocolate, melted
1 cup whipping cream, whipped

Combine coconut, nuts, flour and margarine; press onto bottom and sides of 9-inch pie plate. Bake at 325°, 10 minutes. Cool.

Combine softened cream cheese, sugar and chocolate, mixing until well blended. Fold in whipped cream. Pour into crust; chill several hours or overnight. Garnish with additional toasted coconut, if desired.

Cherry Cheese Chocolate Pie

1½ cups chocolate wafer crumbs
¼ cup Parkay margarine, melted

     *   *   *

1 8-oz. pkg. Philadelphia Brand cream cheese
½ cup sugar

2 tablespoons milk
½ teaspoon vanilla
1 1-oz. square unsweetened chocolate, melted
½ cup whipping cream, whipped
1 21-oz. can cherry pie filling

Combine crumbs and margarine; press onto bottom and sides of 9-inch pie plate. Bake at 375°, 8 minutes. Cool.

Combine softened cream cheese, sugar, milk and vanilla, mixing until well blended. Divide mixture in half. Blend chocolate into one half; fold whipped cream into second half. Pour chocolate mixture into crust; top with half of pie filling, whipped cream mixture and remaining pie filling. Chill several hours or overnight.

Ambrosia Pie

1 8-oz. pkg. Philadelphia
　Brand cream cheese
½ cup sugar
1 tablespoon lemon juice
2 teaspoons grated lemon
　rind
1 cup whipping cream,
　whipped

½ cup shredded coconut
1½ cups orange sections,
　well-drained
1½ cups banana slices
½ cup Kraft orange
　marmalade

Combine softened cream cheese, sugar, lemon juice and rind, mixing until well blended. Fold in whipped cream and coconut. Spread mixture onto bottom and sides of 9-inch pie plate. Freeze. Combine fruit and marmalade; mix lightly. Let stand 5 minutes. Fill center of cream cheese shell with fruit. Serve immediately.

Mandarin Fruit Pie

1½ cups graham cracker
　crumbs
¼ cup sugar
⅓ cup Parkay margarine,
　melted
　　*　　*　　*
2 8-oz. pkgs. Philadelphia
　Brand cream cheese
⅓ cup sugar

½ teaspoon vanilla
2 eggs
¼ cup Kraft orange
　marmalade
1 20-oz. can crushed
　pineapple, well-drained
1 11-oz. can mandarin
　orange segments, drained

Combine crumbs, sugar and margarine; press onto bottom and sides of 9-inch pie plate.

Combine softened cream cheese, sugar and vanilla, mixing until well blended. Blend in eggs. Stir in marmalade; pour into crust. Bake at 350°, 45 minutes. Cool. Top with pineapple and orange segments.

Pecan Tassies — page 143
Chocolate-Orange Cookies — page 142
Apricot Cream Cheese Cookies — page 142

Pecan Tassies

Miniature pecan tarts in delicate cream cheese pastry — a Kraft classic.

½ **cup Parkay margarine**	¾ **cup packed brown sugar**
1 **3-oz. pkg. Philadelphia Brand cream cheese**	1 **egg**
	1 **teaspoon vanilla**
1 **cup flour**	¾ **cup chopped pecans**

Combine margarine and softened cream cheese, mixing until well blended. Add flour; mix well. Chill. Combine brown sugar, egg and vanilla; mix well. Stir in nuts. Divide dough into twenty-four balls; press into miniature muffin pans. Fill each cup 3/4 full of brown sugar mixture. Bake at 325°, 25 to 30 minutes or until lightly browned. Cool 5 minutes; remove from pan. Sprinkle with confectioners' sugar, if desired.

2 dozen

Chocolate-Orange Cookies

A great flavor combination — chocolate, orange, coconut and cream cheese. Keep the cookie jar filled.

1 **8-oz. pkg. Philadelphia Brand cream cheese**	2 **teaspoons grated orange rind**
1 **cup Parkay margarine**	1 **teaspoon vanilla**
1 **cup sugar**	2¾ **cups flour**
2 **1-oz. squares unsweetened chocolate, melted**	1 **teaspoon baking powder**
	1 **cup shredded coconut**
1 **egg**	

Combine softened cream cheese, margarine and sugar, mixing until well blended. Blend in chocolate, egg, orange rind and vanilla. Add combined flour and baking powder; mix well. Stir in coconut. Drop rounded teaspoonfuls of dough onto greased cookie sheet. Bake at 325°, 15 minutes.

5 dozen

Apricot Cream Cheese Cookies

A lemon-flavored "thumbprint" cookie filled with apricot preserves — a family favorite that is pretty enough for parties.

1½ cups Parkay margarine
1½ cups sugar
1 8-oz. pkg. Philadelphia Brand cream cheese
2 eggs
2 tablespoons lemon juice
1½ teaspoons grated lemon rind
4½ cups flour
1½ teaspoons baking powder
Kraft apricot preserves
Confectioners' sugar

Combine margarine, sugar and softened cream cheese, mixing until well blended. Blend in eggs, lemon juice and rind. Add combined dry ingredients; mix well. Chill. Shape level tablespoonfuls of dough into balls. Place on ungreased cookie sheet; flatten slightly. Indent centers; fill with preserves. Bake at 350°, 15 minutes. Cool; sprinkle with confectioners' sugar.

7 dozen

Banana Raisin Bars

These spicy banana bars are a great after-school treat for active youngsters.

1½ cups packed brown sugar
1 8-oz. pkg. Philadelphia Brand cream cheese
½ cup Parkay margarine
1 cup mashed banana
¼ cup milk
1 egg
2¼ cups flour
1½ teaspoons baking powder
1 teaspoon salt
1 teaspoon cinnamon
1 cup chopped nuts
½ cup raisins
Confectioners' sugar

Combine brown sugar, softened cream cheese and margarine, mixing until well blended. Blend in banana, milk and egg. Add combined dry ingredients; mix well. Stir in nuts and raisins. Pour into greased 15-1/2 × 10-1/2-inch jelly roll pan. Bake at 350°, 30 to 35 minutes or until wooden pick inserted in center comes out clean. Cool. Sprinkle with confectioners' sugar; cut into bars.

Chocolate Chipper Bars

Chewy, chocolate-nut oatmeal bars — always nice to have around the house for unexpected guests or for tucking into brown bag lunches.

1 **8-oz. pkg. Philadelphia Brand cream cheese**	1 **cup old fashioned or quick oats, uncooked**
½ **cup Parkay margarine**	⅔ **cup flour**
½ **cup packed brown sugar**	½ **teaspoon baking powder**
¼ **cup granulated sugar**	¼ **teaspoon salt**
1 **egg**	1 **6-oz. pkg. semi-sweet chocolate pieces**
1 **teaspoon vanilla**	¼ **cup chopped nuts**

Combine softened cream cheese, margarine and sugars, mixing until well blended. Blend in egg and vanilla. Add combined dry ingredients; mix well. Stir in chocolate pieces and nuts. Pour into greased 13 × 9-inch baking pan. Bake at 350°, 30 minutes. Cool; cut into bars.

Fudgy Nut Squares

A no-bake bar cookie — a chocolate coconut crumb crust topped with sweetened cream cheese and a chocolate glaze.

1 **cup Parkay margarine**	½ **cup chopped nuts**
1 **6-oz. pkg. semi-sweet chocolate pieces**	1 **8-oz. pkg. Philadelphia Brand cream cheese**
1¾ **cups graham cracker crumbs**	½ **cup sugar**
1 **cup flaked coconut**	1 **teaspoon vanilla**

In saucepan, combine 3/4 cup margarine and 1/3 cup chocolate pieces; stir over low heat until smooth. Add combined crumbs, coconut and nuts; mix well. Press onto bottom of ungreased 15-1/2 × 10-1/2-inch jelly roll pan. Chill. Combine softened cream cheese, sugar and vanilla, mixing until well blended. Spread over crust; chill. Melt remaining margarine and chocolate pieces; spread over cream cheese layer. Chill; cut into squares.

Lemon Nut Bars

A crisp oatmeal crust topped with a pleasingly tart, lemon cream cheese layer — c'est magnifique.

1⅓ cups flour
  1 cup old fashioned or
     quick oats, uncooked
  ½ cup packed brown sugar
  ¼ cup granulated sugar
  ½ teaspoon salt
  ¾ cup Parkay margarine

  ½ cup chopped nuts
        *   *   *
  1 8-oz. pkg. Philadelphia
     Brand cream cheese
  1 egg
  2 tablespoons lemon juice
  1 teaspoon grated lemon rind

Combine flour, oats, sugars and salt; cut in margarine until mixture resembles coarse crumbs. Stir in nuts. Reserve 1 cup; press remaining crumb mixture onto bottom of greased 13 × 9-inch baking pan. Bake at 350°, 15 minutes.

Combine softened cream cheese and egg, mixing until well blended. Blend in lemon juice and rind. Pour over crust; sprinkle with reserved crumb mixture. Bake at 350°, 25 minutes. Cool; cut into bars.

Orange Almond Cookies

  1 8-oz. pkg. Philadelphia
     Brand cream cheese
  1 cup Parkay margarine
  ⅔ cup sugar

  2 tablespoons grated orange
     rind
  ½ teaspoon almond extract
  2 cups flour
     Whole blanched almonds

Combine softened cream cheese, margarine and sugar, mixing until well blended. Blend in orange rind and extract. Add flour; mix well. Chill. Shape rounded tablespoonfuls of dough into balls. Place on ungreased cookie sheet; press almond into top of each ball. Bake at 400°, 15 minutes.

4 dozen

Marble Squares

1 8-oz. pkg. Philadelphia Brand cream cheese
2⅓ cups sugar
3 eggs
¾ cup water
½ cup Parkay margarine
1½ 1-oz. squares unsweetened chocolate

2 cups flour
½ cup dairy sour cream
1 teaspoon baking soda
½ teaspoon salt
1 6-oz. pkg. semi-sweet chocolate pieces

Combine softened cream cheese and 1/3 cup sugar, mixing until well blended. Blend in one egg. In saucepan, combine water, margarine and chocolate; bring to boil. Remove from heat. Add combined remaining sugar and flour; mix well. Blend in remaining eggs, sour cream, baking soda and salt. Pour into greased and floured 15-1/2 × 10-1/2-inch jelly roll pan. Spoon cream cheese mixture over chocolate batter. Cut through batter with knife several times for marble effect; sprinkle with chocolate pieces. Bake at 375°, 25 to 30 minutes or until wooden pick inserted in center comes out clean. Cool; cut into squares.

Nutty Coconut Drops

1¼ cups sugar
1 8-oz. pkg. Philadelphia Brand cream cheese
1 cup Parkay margarine
1 egg
2 tablespoons milk

¼ teaspoon vanilla
1½ cups flour
1 cup flaked coconut, toasted
Chopped nuts

Combine sugar, softened cream cheese and margarine, mixing until well blended. Blend in egg, milk and vanilla. Add flour; mix well. Stir in coconut. Drop rounded teaspoonfuls of dough onto ungreased cookie sheet. Sprinkle with nuts. Bake at 325°, 18 to 20 minutes or until edges are lightly browned. Cool slightly before removing from cookie sheet.

Approximately 5 dozen

Marble Squares

Princess Brownies

A perennial favorite, brownies from a mix dressed up with a luscious marbling of sweetened cream cheese — always popular and very easy.

1 pkg. family size brownie mix
1 8-oz. pkg. Philadelphia Brand cream cheese
⅓ cup sugar
1 egg
½ teaspoon vanilla

Prepare brownie mix as directed on package. Combine softened cream cheese and sugar, mixing until well blended. Blend in egg and vanilla. Reserve 1/2 cup brownie batter; spread remaining batter onto bottom of greased 13 × 9-inch baking pan. Cover with cream cheese mixture; spoon on reserved batter. Cut through batter with knife several times for marble effect. Bake at 350°, 35 to 40 minutes. Cool; cut into squares.

"Philly" Chippers

1 8-oz. pkg. Philadelphia Brand cream cheese
1 cup Parkay margarine
¾ cup granulated sugar
¾ cup packed brown sugar
1 egg
1 teaspoon vanilla
2½ cups flour
1 teaspoon baking powder
½ teaspoon salt
1 12-oz. pkg. semi-sweet chocolate pieces
½ cup chopped nuts

Combine softened cream cheese, margarine and sugars, mixing until well blended. Blend in egg and vanilla. Add combined dry ingredients; mix well. Stir in chocolate pieces and nuts. Drop rounded teaspoonfuls of dough onto greased cookie sheet. Bake at 375°, 15 to 18 minutes or until lightly browned.

Approximately 5-1/2 dozen

"Philly" Sugar Cookies

1 8-oz. pkg. Philadelphia
Brand cream cheese
1 cup Parkay margarine

Sugar
½ teaspoon rum flavoring
2 cups flour

Combine softened cream cheese, margarine, 2/3 cup sugar and flavoring, mixing until well blended. Add flour; mix well. Chill several hours or overnight. Shape rounded tea-spoonfuls of dough into balls; roll in sugar. Place on ungreased cookie sheet; flatten slightly. Bake at 350°, 12 minutes.

Approximately 5 dozen

Cocoa Drops

1½ cups sugar
1 8-oz. pkg. Philadelphia
Brand cream cheese
1 cup Parkay margarine
1 egg

1 teaspoon vanilla
2¼ cups flour
½ cup cocoa
1 teaspoon baking powder

Combine sugar, softened cream cheese and margarine, mix-ing until well blended. Blend in egg and vanilla. Add com-bined dry ingredients; mix well. Drop rounded teaspoonfuls of dough onto greased cookie sheet. Bake at 375°, 12 minutes.

Approximately 4-1/2 dozen

Cream Cheese Spritz

1 8-oz. pkg. Philadelphia
Brand cream cheese
1 cup Parkay margarine

⅔ cup sugar
1 teaspoon vanilla
1¾ cups flour

Combine softened cream cheese, margarine, sugar and vanilla, mixing until well blended. Add flour; mix well. Chill. Force dough through cookie press onto ungreased cookie sheet. Bake at 400°, 6 to 8 minutes or until set and very lightly browned.

Approximately 9 dozen

Lemon Glazed Jam Bars

Chewy cream cheese jam bars with a lemon glaze.

1 **8-oz. pkg. Philadelphia Brand cream cheese**
½ **cup Parkay margarine**
½ **cup packed brown sugar**
½ **cup granulated sugar**
1 **10-oz. jar Kraft apricot or peach preserves**
2 **eggs**
1 **teaspoon vanilla**
1¾ **cups flour**

1 **teaspoon baking powder**
½ **teaspoon baking soda**
¼ **teaspoon salt**
½ **cup chopped nuts**
    *   *   *
1½ **cups sifted confectioners' sugar**
2 **tablespoons milk**
1 **tablespoon lemon juice**

Combine softened cream cheese, margarine and sugars, mixing until well blended. Blend in preserves, eggs and vanilla. Add combined dry ingredients; mix well. Stir in nuts. Pour into greased and floured 15-1/2 × 10-1/2-inch jelly roll pan. Bake at 350°, 30 to 35 minutes or until wooden pick inserted in center comes out clean. Cool slightly.

Combine confectioners' sugar, milk and lemon juice; mix well. Drizzle over warm bars. Cool; cut into bars.

Shortbread Cookies

1½ **cups Parkay margarine**
1 **8-oz. pkg. Philadelphia Brand cream cheese**

½ **cup sugar**
3 **cups flour**
   Confectioners' sugar

Combine margarine, softened cream cheese and sugar, mixing until well blended. Add flour; mix well. Shape level teaspoonfuls of dough into balls; place on greased cookie sheet. Bake at 400°, 10 to 12 minutes or until edges are lightly browned. Cool; sprinkle with confectioners' sugar.

Approximately 7 dozen

Chocolate ''Philly'' Fudge — page 152
Tea Party Tarts — page 153
Fruit Dreams — page 152

Chocolate "Philly" Fudge

A Kraft original and one of our most requested recipes.

4 cups sifted confectioners'
   sugar
1 8-oz. pkg. Philadelphia
   Brand cream cheese

4 1-oz. squares unsweetened
   chocolate, melted
½ cup chopped nuts
1 teaspooon vanilla
   Dash of salt

Gradually add sugar to softened cream cheese, mixing well after each addition. Add remaining ingredients; mix well. Spread into greased 8-inch square pan. Chill several hours or overnight; cut into squares. Garnish with additional nuts, if desired.

1-3/4 pounds

Variations: Omit nuts and vanilla; add few drops peppermint extract and 1/4 cup crushed peppermint candy.
Omit nuts; add 1 cup shredded coconut.
Omit nuts; add 1/2 cup chopped maraschino cherries.

Fruit Dreams

Very French and very festive, these fruit creme tarts can be the highlight of any party. Make the tart shells in advance and fill just before serving.

1 8-oz. pkg. Philadelphia
   Brand cream cheese
½ cup sugar
1 teaspoon brandy extract

1 teaspoon lemon juice
1 cup whipping cream,
   whipped
   Assorted fresh fruit

Combine softened cream cheese, sugar, extract and lemon juice, mixing until well blended. Fold in whipped cream. Spoon mixture onto waxed paper covered cookie sheet to form eight shells; freeze. Fill center of each shell with fruit before serving.

8 servings

Variation: Substitute 21-oz. can cherry pie filling for fresh fruit.

Tea Party Tarts

These creme filled tarts are elegant, easy and complementary to a wide variety of fruit toppings.

1 **cup flour**	½ **cup sugar**
¼ **teaspoon salt**	2 **tablespoons cornstarch**
1 **8-oz. pkg. Philadelphia**	**Dash of salt**
Brand cream cheese,	1 **cup milk**
cut in half	½ **teaspoon vanilla**
⅔ **cup Parkay margarine**	**Strawberry halves**
* * *	**Banana slices**

Combine flour and salt; cut in half of cream cheese and margarine until mixture resembles coarse crumbs. Divide dough into twelve balls; chill. On lightly floured surface, roll out each ball to 4-1/2-inch circle. Place in 3-inch tart pans; prick bottom with fork. Bake at 375°, 15 to 20 minutes or until golden brown. Cool.

In saucepan, combine sugar, cornstarch and salt. Gradually add milk; cook, stirring constantly, until mixture is clear and thickened. Add vanilla and remaining cream cheese, cubed; stir over low heat until smooth. Fill tarts; chill. Top with fruit before serving.

12 tarts

"Philly" Pound Cake

1½ **cups sugar**	1½ **teaspoons vanilla**
1 **8-oz. pkg. Philadelphia**	4 **eggs**
Brand cream cheese	2 **cups sifted cake flour**
¾ **cup Parkay margarine**	1½ **teaspoons baking powder**

Combine sugar, softened cream cheese, margarine and vanilla, mixing until well blended. Add eggs; mix at low speed on electric mixer until blended. Gradually add flour sifted with baking powder, mixing at low speed until blended. Pour into greased and floured 9 × 5-inch loaf pan. Bake at 325°, 1 hour and 20 minutes. Cool 5 minutes; remove from pan. Sprinkle with confectioners' sugar, if desired.

Cranberry Supreme

1 cup graham cracker crumbs

¼ cup Parkay margarine, melted

* * *

2 cups cranberries

1 cup granulated sugar

½ cup water

¼ cup chopped nuts

2 tablespoons Kraft orange marmalade

* * *

1 8-oz. pkg. Philadelphia Brand cream cheese

⅓ cup sifted confectioners' sugar

1 tablespoon milk

1 teaspoon vanilla

1 cup whipping cream, whipped

Combine crumbs and margarine; press onto bottom of 8-inch square baking pan.

Combine cranberries, granulated sugar and water. Bring to boil; simmer 20 minutes. Stir in nuts and marmalade; chill.

Combine softened cream cheese, confectioners' sugar, milk and vanilla, mixing until well blended. Fold in whipped cream. Spoon over crust; top with cranberry mixture. Chill several hours or overnight.

8 servings

Seafoam Lime Dessert

1 3-oz. pkg. lime flavored gelatin

1 cup boiling water

½ cup cold water

1 tablespoon lemon juice

1 8-oz. pkg. Philadelphia Brand cream cheese

2 8¼-oz. cans crushed pineapple, drained

1½ cups Kraft miniature marshmallows

½ cup chopped nuts

Dissolve gelatin in boiling water; add cold water and lemon juice. Gradually add to softened cream cheese, mixing until well blended. Chill until partially set; fold in remaining ingredients. Pour into 8-inch square baking dish; chill until firm.

6 servings

Bavarian Apple Torte

½ **cup Parkay margarine**
⅓ **cup sugar**
¼ **teaspoon vanilla**
1 **cup flour**
    *   *   *
1 **8-oz. pkg. Philadelphia**
   Brand cream cheese
¼ **cup sugar**

1 **egg**
½ **teaspoon vanilla**
   *   *   *
4 **cups thin peeled apple**
   slices
⅓ **cup sugar**
½ **teaspoon cinnamon**
¼ **cup sliced almonds**

Cream margarine and sugar until light and fluffy. Blend in vanilla. Add flour; mix well. Spread dough onto bottom and 1-1/2-inches high around sides of 9-inch springform pan.

Combine softened cream cheese and sugar, mixing until well blended. Blend in egg and vanilla; pour into pastry-lined pan.

Toss apples with combined sugar and cinnamon. Spoon apple mixture over cream cheese layer; sprinkle with nuts. Bake at 450°, 10 minutes. Reduce oven temperature to 400°; continue baking 25 minutes. Loosen cake from rim of pan. Cool; remove rim. Chill.

Chocolate "Philly" Frosting

A famous Kraft favorite, this easy cream cheese frosting is readily adaptable to many variations.

1 **8-oz. pkg. Philadelphia**
   Brand cream cheese
1 **tablespoon milk**
1 **teaspoon vanilla**
   Dash of salt

5 **cups sifted confectioners'**
   sugar
3 **1-oz. squares unsweetened**
   chocolate, melted

Combine softened cream cheese, milk, vanilla and salt, mixing until well blended. Gradually add sugar, mixing well after each addition. Blend in chocolate.

Fills and frosts two 8 or 9-inch cake layers

Caramel Puff Pancake

A high-rising baked pancake that's so easy to make and looks magnificent!

28 Kraft caramels	2 eggs
¼ cup water	½ cup flour
4 cups peeled apple slices	¼ teaspoon salt
* * *	½ cup milk
1 7-oz. jar Kraft marshmallow creme	1 tablespoon Parkay margarine
1 8-oz. pkg. Philadelphia Brand cream cheese	
* * *	

Melt caramels with water in saucepan over low heat. Stir occasionally until sauce is smooth. Add apples; heat thoroughly.

Gradually add marshmallow creme to softened cream cheese, mixing until well blended.

Combine eggs, flour, salt and milk; beat until smooth. Heat heavy oven-proof 9-inch skillet at 450° until very hot. Coat skillet with margarine; immediately add batter. Bake on lowest shelf in oven at 450°, 10 minutes. Reduce oven temperature to 350°; continue baking 10 minutes or until golden brown. Fill with fruit; top with cream cheese mixture. Serve immediately.

6 to 8 servings

Variation: Substitute 29-oz. can peach slices, drained or 30-oz. can apricot halves, drained, for apples.

Cherry Cheese Delight

A great make-ahead dessert — pineapple, blueberry or peach pie filling can be substituted for cherry.

1¼ cups graham cracker crumbs

⅓ cup Parkay margarine, melted

* * *

1 8-oz. pkg. Philadelphia Brand cream cheese

½ cup sifted confectioners' sugar

1 tablespoon milk

¼ teaspoon almond extract

½ cup chopped pecans

* * *

¼ cup sifted confectioners' sugar

1 cup whipping cream

1 21-oz. can cherry pie filling

¼ teaspoon almond extract

Combine crumbs and margarine; press onto bottom of 9-inch square baking pan.

Combine softened cream cheese, sugar, milk and extract, mixing until well blended. Spread over crust; sprinkle with nuts.

Gradually add sugar to cream, beating until stiff peaks form. Spread over nuts. Combine pie filling and extract; spread over whipped cream. Chill several hours or overnight.

8 to 10 servings

Vanilla "Philly" Fudge

8 cups sifted confectioners' sugar

1 8-oz. pkg. Philadelphia Brand cream cheese

1½ teaspoons vanilla

Dash of salt

Gradually add sugar to softened cream cheese, mixing well after each addition. Stir in vanilla and salt. Spread into greased 8-inch square baking pan. Chill several hours or overnight; cut into squares.

2 pounds

Chocolate Soufflé

2 envelopes unflavored
  gelatin
2¼ cups cold water
1½ cups sugar
4 eggs, separated
1 8-oz. pkg. Philadelphia
  Brand cream cheese

3 1-oz. squares unsweetened
  chocolate, melted
½ teaspoon almond extract
1 cup whipping cream,
  whipped

Soften gelatin in 1 cup cold water; stir over low heat until dissolved. Add remaining cold water; remove from heat. Blend in 1 cup sugar and beaten egg yolks; cook 3 minutes over low heat, stirring constantly until thickened. Combine softened cream cheese and chocolate, mixing until well blended. Gradually add gelatin, mixing until blended. Stir in extract. Chill until slightly thickened. Beat egg whites until foamy; gradually add remaining sugar, beating until stiff peaks form. Fold egg whites and whipped cream into cream cheese mixture. Wrap 3-inch collar of aluminum foil around top of 1-1/2-quart soufflé dish; secure with tape. Pour mixture into dish; chill until firm. Remove collar before serving. Garnish with toasted sliced almonds, if desired.

8 to 10 servings

Vanilla "Philly" Frosting

1 8-oz. pkg. Philadelphia
  Brand cream cheese
1 tablespoon milk

1 teaspoon vanilla
5½ cups sifted confectioners'
  sugar

Combine softened cream cheese, milk and vanilla, mixing until well blended. Gradually add sugar, mixing well after each addition.

Fills and frosts two 8 or 9-inch cake layers

Variations: Substitute 1 teaspoon almond extract for vanilla.
           Stir in 1/4 cup crushed peppermint candy.
           Stir in 1/4 cup chopped maraschino cherries and
           few drops red food coloring.

Chocolate Soufflé

"Philly" Marble Cake

1½ cups granulated sugar
1 8-oz. pkg. Philadelphia
  Brand cream cheese
1 cup Parkay margarine
1½ teaspoons vanilla
4 eggs
2¼ cups sifted cake flour
1½ teaspoons baking powder
2 1-oz. squares unsweetened
  chocolate, melted

½ teaspoon baking soda
*   *   *
2 tablespoons Parkay
  margarine
2 tablespoons milk
1½ cups sifted confectioners'
  sugar
½ teaspoon vanilla

Combine granulated sugar, softened cream cheese, margarine and vanilla, mixing until well blended. Add eggs, one at a time, mixing well after each addition. Gradually add sifted cake flour and baking powder; mix well. Reserve 2 cups batter. Add chocolate and baking soda to remaining batter; mix well. Spoon chocolate and vanilla batter alternately into greased and floured 10-inch tube pan; cut through batter with knife several times for marble effect. Bake at 325°, 1 hour. Cool 5 minutes; remove from pan.

Heat margarine and milk in saucepan. Add confectioners' sugar; mix well. Stir in vanilla. Drizzle over warm cake.

Coffee "Philly" Frosting

A creamy coffee frosting that is especially compatible with chocolate, spice or nut cakes.

4½ cups sifted confectioners'
  sugar
1 8-oz. pkg. Philadelphia
  Brand cream cheese

2 teaspoons instant coffee
  powder

Gradually add sugar to softened cream cheese, mixing well after each addition. Add coffee powder; mix well.

Fills and frosts two 8 or 9-inch cake layers

Creme à la Maison

This cream cheese version of Bavarian cream is extra special topped with a delicate apricot sauce.

1 envelope unflavored gelatin	½ teaspoon vanilla
	Dash of salt
¼ cup cold water	1 cup milk
1 8-oz. pkg. Philadelphia Brand cream cheese	1 cup whipping cream, whipped
½ cup sugar	Apricot Wine Sauce

Soften gelatin in cold water; stir over low heat until dissolved. Combine softened cream cheese, sugar, vanilla and salt, mixing until well blended. Gradually add milk and gelatin, mixing until blended. Chill until slightly thickened. Fold in whipped cream. Pour into lightly oiled 1-quart mold; chill until firm. Unmold. Serve with:

Apricot Wine Sauce

1 10-oz. jar Kraft apricot preserves	⅓ cup dry white wine

Combine ingredients; mix well. Chill.

6 to 8 servings

Holiday Gift Cake

1½ cups granulated sugar
1 8-oz. pkg. Philadelphia Brand cream cheese
1 cup Parkay margarine
1½ teaspoons vanilla
4 eggs
2¼ cups sifted cake flour
1½ teaspoons baking powder

¾ cup well-drained chopped maraschino cherries
½ cup chopped pecans
* * *
½ cup finely chopped pecans
1½ cups sifted confectioners' sugar
2 tablespoons milk

Combine granulated sugar, softened cream cheese, margarine and vanilla, mixing until well blended. Add eggs, one at a time, mixing well after each addition. Gradually add 2 cups flour sifted with baking powder, mixing well after each addition. Toss remaining flour with cherries and chopped nuts; fold into batter.

Sprinkle greased 10-inch tube pan with nuts; pour batter into pan. Bake at 325°, 1 hour and 20 minutes. Cool 5 minutes; remove from pan. Cool thoroughly. Combine confectioners' sugar and milk; mix well. Drizzle over cake; garnish with additional cherries and nuts, if desired.

Variations: Omit finely chopped nuts. Pour batter into three greased and floured 1-lb. coffee cans. Bake at 325°, 1 hour.

Omit finely chopped nuts. Pour batter into four greased and floured 1-lb. shortening cans. Bake at 325°, 1 hour.

Omit finely chopped nuts. Pour batter into twelve greased and floured 8-oz. tomato sauce cans. Bake at 325°, 25 minutes.

Omit finely chopped nuts. Pour batter into five greased and floured 5-3/4 × 3-1/4-inch loaf pans. Bake at 325°, 45 to 50 minutes or until wooden pick inserted in center comes out clean.

Make Ahead: Prepare as directed. Wrap securely; freeze. When ready to serve, thaw wrapped at room temperature for 24 hours.

Heavenly Cream Soufflé

2 envelopes unflavored
   gelatin
2 cups cold water
1 cup sugar
4 eggs, separated
1 8-oz. pkg. Philadelphia
   Brand cream cheese

¼ cup white creme de cocoa
1 cup whipping cream,
   whipped
1 16-oz. can peach slices,
   drained

Soften gelatin in 1 cup cold water; stir over low heat until dissolved. Add remaining cold water. Remove from heat; blend in 3/4 cup sugar and beaten egg yolks. Cook 3 minutes over low heat, stirring constantly until thickened. Gradually add to softened cream cheese, mixing until well blended. Stir in creme de cocoa. Chill until slightly thickened. Beat egg whites until foamy. Gradually add remaining sugar, beating until stiff peaks form. Fold egg whites and whipped cream into cream cheese mixture. Wrap 3-inch collar of aluminum foil around top of 1-1/2-quart soufflé dish; secure with tape. Pour mixture into dish; chill until firm. Remove collar before serving. Serve with peach slices.

8 to 10 servings

Coconut "Philly" Fudge Balls

5 cups sifted confectioners'
   sugar
1 8-oz. pkg. Philadelphia
   Brand cream cheese

1 8-oz. pkg. shredded
   coconut
½ teaspoon vanilla
   Dash of salt

Gradually add sugar to softened cream cheese, mixing well after each addition. Add 1 cup coconut, vanilla and salt; mix well. Chill. Shape into balls; roll in remaining coconut. Chill several hours or overnight.

Approximately 3 dozen

"Philly" Fruit Pizza

1 18-oz. roll refrigerated
   sugar slice-and-bake
   cookies
   *   *   *
1 8-oz. container soft
   Philadelphia Brand
   cream cheese

⅓ cup sugar
½ teaspoon vanilla
   Assorted fruits
½ cup Kraft orange
   marmalade, peach or
   apricot preserves
2 tablespoons water

Cut cookie dough into 1/8-inch slices. Arrange cookie slices, slightly overlapping, on aluminum foil covered 14-inch pizza pan; press edges to seal. Bake at 375°, 10 to 12 minutes or until golden brown. Cool; remove from foil onto serving plate.

Combine cream cheese, sugar and vanilla, mixing until well blended. Spread over crust. Arrange fruit on cream cheese mixture. Glaze with combined marmalade and water. Chill. Cut into wedges.

Creamy "Philly" Frosting

Easy to blend and spread, this quick frosting is extra smooth made with soft cream cheese.

1 8-oz. container soft
   Philadelphia Brand
   cream cheese
2 tablespoons Parkay
   margarine

½ teaspoon vanilla
   Dash of salt
5 cups sifted confectioners'
   sugar

Combine cream cheese, margarine, vanilla and salt, mixing until well blended. Gradually add sugar, mixing well after each addition.

Fills and frosts two 8 or 9-inch cake layers

Variations: Substitute 1-1/2 teaspoons lemon juice and 1
            teaspoon grated lemon rind for vanilla.
            Add 1/4 cup cocoa to cream cheese mixture
            before adding sugar; mix well.

"Philly" Fruit Pizza

Pineapple Cheesecake Dessert

A touch of the tropics — a crisp coconut crust topped with a fluffy pineapple cream cheese filling.

1½ cups shredded coconut
½ cup chopped nuts
2 tablespoons flour
2 tablespoons Parkay margarine, melted
    *   *   *
1 envelope unflavored gelatin

¼ cup cold water
1 20-oz. can crushed pineapple, undrained
3 eggs, separated
½ cup sugar
3 8-oz. containers soft Philadelphia Brand cream cheese

Combine coconut, nuts, flour and margarine; press onto bottom of 13 × 9-inch baking dish. Bake at 350°, 15 minutes. Cool.

Soften gelatin in cold water. Drain pineapple, reserving 1/2 cup syrup. Combine syrup, egg yolks and 1/4 cup sugar; cook over medium heat 5 minutes, stirring constantly until thickened. Add gelatin; stir until dissolved. Gradually add to cream cheese, mixing until well blended. Chill until slightly thickened. Beat egg whites until foamy; gradually add remaining sugar, beating until stiff peaks form. Fold pineapple and egg whites into cream cheese mixture. Pour over crust; chill until firm.

8 to 10 servings

Coconut Torte

1 8-oz. container soft Philadelphia Brand cream cheese
¼ cup sugar
1 tablespoon Kraft pasteurized orange juice

½ cup coconut, toasted
¼ cup sliced almonds, toasted
1 9-inch yellow cake layer

Combine cream cheese, sugar and orange juice, mixing until well blended. Add coconut and nuts; mix well. Cut cake in half horizontally. Spread cake layers with frosting; stack. Garnish with additional toasted coconut, if desired. Chill.

"Philly" Banana Pudding

Great for the kids and easy for mom — prepare in a jiffy and serve later.

12 vanilla wafer cookies	½ teaspoon vanilla
1 8-oz. container soft Philadelphia Brand cream cheese	1 cup whipping cream, whipped
¼ cup sugar	2 medium bananas, sliced

Line bottom and sides of 1-quart bowl with cookies. Combine cream cheese, sugar and vanilla, mixing until well blended. Fold in remaining ingredients. Spoon over cookies; chill.

4 to 6 servings

Regal Banana Crepes

Crepes can be completely prepared several hours in advance and refrigerated. When ready to serve, simply spoon on hot fudge topping.

3 eggs, beaten	3 tablespoons sugar
⅔ cup flour	2 tablespoons milk
½ teaspoon salt	½ teaspoon vanilla
¾ cup milk	1 medium banana, sliced
* * *	Kraft fudge topping,
1 8-oz. container soft Philadelphia Brand cream cheese	heated

Combine eggs, flour, salt and milk; beat until smooth. Let stand 30 minutes. For each crepe, pour 1/4 cup batter into hot, lightly greased 8-inch skillet. Cook on one side only until underside is lightly browned.

Combine cream cheese, sugar, milk and vanilla, mixing until well blended. Fill each crepe with approximately 3 tablespoons cream cheese mixture; top with banana slices. Roll up. Spoon topping over crepes.

6 crepes

Creamy Rice Dessert

A creamy fruit and rice dessert that's bound to become a family favorite — a great "do-ahead" for hectic days when there's no time to cook.

1 8¼-oz. can crushed pineapple, undrained
2 cups cooked rice, chilled
1 11-oz. can mandarin orange segments, drained
½ cup maraschino cherry halves
½ cup chopped nuts
1 8-oz. container soft Philadelphia Brand cream cheese
¼ cup sugar
¼ teaspoon vanilla

Drain pineapple, reserving 3 tablespoons syrup. Combine rice, pineapple, orange segments, cherries and nuts; mix lightly. Combine reserved syrup, cream cheese, sugar and vanilla, mixing until well blended. Add to rice mixture; mix lightly.

6 servings

Chocolate Angel Pudding

1 8-oz. container soft Philadelphia Brand cream cheese
½ cup sugar
½ teaspoon rum flavoring
1 1-oz. square unsweetened chocolate, melted
3½ cups 1-inch angel food cake cubes
1 cup whipping cream, whipped

Combine cream cheese, sugar and flavoring, mixing until well blended. Blend in chocolate. Stir in cake cubes; fold in whipped cream. Spoon into 1-quart bowl. Chill. Garnish with sliced fruit and nuts, if desired.

4 to 6 servings

Chicken Corn Pies — page 174
Cucumber 'n Onion Salad — page 171

Sherried Spread

1 3-oz. pkg. Philadelphia Brand cream cheese	2 teaspoons sherry
	1 tablespoon chopped pecans

Combine softened cream cheese and sherry, mixing until well blended. Stir in nuts. Serve with party rye or pumpernickel bread slices.

1/2 cup

Appetizing Tortillas

1 3-oz. pkg. Philadelphia Brand cream cheese	4 flour tortillas
2 tablespoons chopped green chili peppers	2 tablespoons Parkay margarine, melted
Dash of onion salt	Taco sauce

Combine softened cream cheese, chili peppers and onion salt, mixing until well blended. Spread on tortillas; roll up. Place on ungreased cookie sheet; brush with margarine. Bake at 350°, 20 minutes. Serve with taco sauce.

4 appetizers

Zesty Dip

Great for quick snacks — tote this colorful dip to picnics.

1 3-oz. pkg. Philadelphia Brand cream cheese	2 tablespoons shredded carrot
¼ cup dairy sour cream	1 tablespoon milk
2 tablespoons chopped radishes	¼ teaspoon Worcestershire sauce
	¼ teaspoon salt

Combine softened cream cheese and sour cream, mixing until well blended. Add remaining ingredients; mix well. Chill. Serve with vegetable dippers or chips.

3/4 cup

Cucumber 'n Onion Salad

1 3-oz. pkg. Philadelphia
    Brand cream cheese
¼ cup dairy sour cream
¼ teaspoon celery seed

Dash of salt
1 cup peeled cucumber slices
½ cup red onion rings

Combine softened cream cheese, sour cream and seasonings, mixing until well blended. Add cucumber and onion; mix lightly. Chill. Toss before serving.

2 servings

Special Ambrosia

1 3-oz. pkg. Philadelphia
    Brand cream cheese
2 tablespoons milk
2 tablespoons sugar
1 teaspoon vanilla

1 medium banana, sliced
1 medium orange, sectioned
1 medium apple, chopped
¼ cup shredded coconut
    Lettuce cups

Combine softened cream cheese, milk, sugar and vanilla, mixing until well blended. Add fruit and coconut; mix lightly. Chill. Serve in lettuce cups.

2 to 4 servings

Potato Chowder

1 cup water
1¼ cups chopped potatoes
2 tablespoons chopped green
    onion
1 3-oz. pkg. Philadelphia
    Brand cream cheese,
    cubed

¼ cup (1 oz.) Kraft grated
    parmesan cheese
¼ cup milk
2 crisply cooked bacon
    slices, crumbled

In saucepan, combine water and vegetables; bring to boil. Cover; simmer 15 minutes or until potatoes are tender. Add remaining ingredients; stir over low heat until cream cheese is melted. Top each serving with additional bacon, if desired.

Two 1-cup servings

Vegetable Rice Soup

1 cup water
½ cup carrot slices
½ cup celery slices
2 tablespoons chopped onion
2 tablespoons rice

¼ teaspoon salt
Dash of pepper
1 3-oz. pkg. Philadelphia
   Brand cream cheese,
   cubed

In saucepan, combine water, vegetables, rice and seasonings; bring to boil. Cover; simmer 15 minutes or until vegetables and rice are tender. Add cream cheese; stir over low heat until melted.

Two 1-cup servings

Super Noodle Side Dish

1 3-oz. pkg. Philadelphia
   Brand cream cheese,
   cubed
¼ cup milk

2 tablespoons chopped green
   onion
Dash of pepper
1 cup (2 ozs.) noodles,
   cooked, drained

Heat cream cheese and milk over low heat; stir until smooth. Stir in onion and pepper; toss with hot noodles.

2 servings

Saucy Broccoli

1 3-oz. pkg. Philadelphia
   Brand cream cheese,
   cubed
¼ cup milk

1 tablespoon Kraft grated
   parmesan cheese
⅛ teaspoon onion powder
1 10-oz. pkg. frozen broccoli
   spears, cooked, drained

Heat cream cheese and milk over low heat; stir until smooth. Stir in parmesan cheese and onion powder. Serve over hot broccoli.

2 servings

Variation: Substitute 10-oz. pkg. frozen cauliflower, cooked, drained, for broccoli.

Stuffed Tomatoes

An attractive party vegetable for year 'round entertaining.

2 medium tomatoes	¼ teaspoon salt
1 8-oz. can peas, drained	Dash of pepper
1 3-oz. pkg. Philadelphia	¼ cup soft bread crumbs
Brand cream cheese,	1 tablespoon Parkay
cubed	margarine, melted

Remove tops of tomatoes; scoop out centers, leaving 1/4-inch shell. Chop enough pulp to measure 1/3 cup; drain. Combine pulp, peas, cream cheese and seasonings; mix lightly. Fill shells with vegetable mixture. Sprinkle tops with combined bread crumbs and margarine. Bake at 375°, 20 minutes.

2 servings

Twice-Baked Potatoes

Twice baked potatoes for two made extra creamy with cream cheese. Sprinkle with parmesan cheese for a special flavor treat.

1 large baked potato	1 3-oz. pkg. Philadelphia
2 tablespoons Parkay	Brand cream cheese,
margarine	cubed
1 tablespoon milk	Paprika
Dash of salt	

Slice potato in half lengthwise; scoop out centers, leaving 1/8-inch shell. Combine potato, margarine, milk and salt; beat until fluffy. Stir in cream cheese. Fill shells; sprinkle with paprika. Place on ungreased cookie sheet. Bake at 375°, 20 minutes.

2 servings

Chicken Corn Pies

A complete meal in a dish — creamed chicken baked over cornbread.

¾ cup cornmeal
¼ cup flour
¼ teaspoon baking powder
¼ teaspoon salt
⅓ cup hot water
1 egg
2 tablespoons Parkay margarine, melted
        *   *   *
1 3-oz. pkg. Philadelphia Brand cream cheese, cubed

2 tablespoons milk
1 egg
1 cup chopped cooked chicken
½ cup (2 ozs.) shredded Kraft sharp cheddar cheese
¼ cup mushroom slices
¼ cup celery slices
2 tablespoons green onion slices
¼ teaspoon salt
Dash of pepper

Combine dry ingredients. Add combined water, egg and margarine, mixing just until moistened. Pour into two lightly greased 6-inch pie plates.

Heat cream cheese and milk over low heat; stir until smooth. Blend in egg. Add remaining ingredients; mix lightly. Spoon over cornmeal mixture. Bake at 350°, 25 to 30 minutes.

2 servings

Chicken Divan

¾ cup milk
1 3-oz. pkg. Philadelphia Brand cream cheese, cubed
½ teaspoon Worcestershire sauce

1 cup broccoli flowerets, cooked, drained
½ cup (2 ozs.) shredded Kraft sharp cheddar cheese
2 chicken breasts, cooked, sliced

Heat milk and cream cheese over low heat; stir until smooth. Stir in Worcestershire sauce. Place broccoli in 10 × 6-inch baking dish. Top with 1/4 cup cheddar cheese, chicken and cream cheese sauce. Bake at 350°, 25 minutes. Top with remaining cheddar cheese; continue baking 5 minutes or until cheddar cheese is melted.

2 servings

Supper Stroganoff

½ lb. round steak, cut into strips
1 tablespoon Parkay margarine
2 tablespoons green onion slices
⅓ cup milk

1 3-oz. pkg. Philadelphia Brand cream cheese, cubed
¼ teaspoon lemon juice
Dash of salt and pepper
1½ cups (3 ozs.) noodles, cooked, drained

Brown meat in margarine. Add onion; cook until tender. Add milk and cream cheese; stir over low heat until cream cheese is melted. Stir in lemon juice and seasonings. Serve over hot noodles.

2 servings

Vegetable Spaghetti

1 cup 1-inch broccoli pieces
½ cup mushroom slices
  Parkay margarine
1 3-oz. pkg. Philadelphia Brand cream cheese, cubed
¼ cup milk

3½ ozs. spaghetti, cooked, drained
½ cup cherry tomato halves
¼ cup (1 oz.) Kraft grated parmesan cheese
¼ teaspoon oregano leaves, crushed

Sauté broccoli and mushrooms in 1 tablespoon margarine. Add cream cheese and milk; stir over low heat until cream cheese is melted. Toss spaghetti with 1 tablespoon margarine; add to cream cheese sauce with combined remaining ingredients. Heat thoroughly.

2 servings

Ham & Cheese Omelet

Omelets are great for leftovers — cooked chicken or turkey are excellent alternatives for ham.

2 tablespoons Parkay margarine
4 eggs, slightly beaten
3 tablespoons milk
Dash of salt and pepper

1 3-oz. pkg. Philadelphia Brand cream cheese, cubed
¼ cup chopped ham
1 tablespoon chopped chives

Melt margarine in 10-inch skillet or omelet pan over low heat. Combine eggs, milk and seasonings; pour into skillet. As egg mixture sets, lift edges slightly with spatula to allow uncooked portion to flow underneath. When set, cover omelet with remaining ingredients. Slip turner underneath, tip skillet to loosen and gently fold in half. Flip over onto serving plate; serve immediately.

2 servings

Mushroom Soufflés

Individual soufflés — how elegant! Serve with a colorful fresh fruit or vegetable salad and croissants.

½ cup mushroom slices
2 tablespoons Parkay margarine
2 tablespoons flour
⅛ teaspoon ground savory
Dash of salt and pepper

½ cup milk
1 3-oz. pkg. Philadelphia Brand cream cheese, cubed
2 eggs, separated

Sauté mushrooms in margarine. Blend in flour and seasonings. Gradually add milk; cook, stirring constantly, until thickened. Add cream cheese; stir over low heat until melted. Remove from heat. Gradually add slightly beaten egg yolks; cool. Fold in stiffly beaten egg whites; pour into two 10-oz. casseroles. With tip of spoon, make slight indentation or "track" around top of soufflés 1-inch in from edge to form a top hat. Bake at 300°, 40 to 45 minutes or until light golden brown. Serve immediately.

2 servings

Philadelphia Poached Eggs

2 3-oz. pkgs. Philadelphia
   Brand cream cheese,
   cubed
¼ cup milk
2 teaspoons lemon juice
   Dash of pepper

2 English muffins, split,
   toasted
4 Canadian-style bacon
   slices, cooked
4 poached eggs

Heat cream cheese and milk over low heat; stir until smooth. Stir in lemon juice and pepper. For each serving, top two muffin halves with bacon, eggs and cream cheese sauce.

2 servings

Stuffed Manicotti

½ lb. ground beef
¼ cup chopped onion
1 3-oz. pkg. Philadelphia
   Brand cream cheese,
   cubed
¼ cup milk
1 teaspoon lemon juice
½ cup (2 ozs.) shredded Kraft
   low moisture part-skim
   mozzarella cheese

   Dash of pepper
4 large manicotti noodles,
   cooked, drained
1 8-oz. can tomato sauce
¼ teaspoon oregano leaves,
   crushed
¼ teaspoon garlic powder

Brown meat; drain. Add onion; cook until tender. Add cream cheese, milk and lemon juice; stir over low heat until cream cheese is melted. Stir in mozzarella cheese and pepper. Fill noodles with meat mixture; place in 8-inch square baking dish. Cover; bake at 350°, 20 minutes. Uncover; top with combined remaining ingredients. Continue baking 10 minutes. Sprinkle with parmesan cheese, if desired.

2 servings

Berry Shortcakes

1 cup flour
2 tablespoons sugar
1½ teaspoons baking powder
¼ teaspoon salt
1 3-oz. pkg. Philadelphia Brand cream cheese, cubed

1 tablespoon Parkay margarine
⅓ cup milk
Strawberry slices
Dairy sour cream

Combine dry ingredients; cut in cream cheese and margarine until mixture resembles coarse crumbs. Add milk, mixing just until moistened. On lightly floured surface, knead dough five times. Shape into two balls; flatten on ungreased cookie sheet. Bake at 425°, 15 minutes. Split shortcakes; fill and top with strawberries and sour cream.

2 servings

Chocolate Cream Pie

½ cup graham cracker crumbs
1 tablespoon sugar
2 tablespoons Parkay margarine, melted
        *   *   *
1 3-oz. pkg. Philadelphia Brand cream cheese

3 tablespoons sugar
1 tablespoon cocoa
1 tablespoon milk
¼ teaspoon vanilla
Dash of cinnamon
½ cup whipping cream, whipped

Combine crumbs, sugar and margarine; press onto bottom and sides of 6-inch pie plate. Bake at 325°, 10 minutes. Cool.

Combine softened cream cheese, sugar, cocoa, milk, vanilla and cinnamon, mixing until well blended. Fold in whipped cream. Pour into crust; chill. Garnish with maraschino cherries, if desired.

2 to 4 servings

Berry Shortcakes

178

Individual Tortes

Dessert for two in a jiffy! Any of your favorite preserves can be substituted for peach.

1   3-oz. pkg. Philadelphia Brand cream cheese

1   tablespoon Parkay margarine

1   teaspoon milk

¼   cup shredded coconut

2   tablespoons chopped nuts

4   pound cake slices

    Kraft peach preserves

Combine softened cream cheese, margarine and milk, mixing until well blended. Add coconut and nuts; mix well. For each serving, spread two cake slices with cream cheese mixture and preserves; stack.

2 servings

Twosome Cheese Pie

This lemon flavored cream cheese pie is delicious "as is" or topped with fresh berries, peach slices or chocolate topping.

½   cup graham cracker crumbs

1   tablespoon sugar

2   tablespoons Parkay margarine, melted

      * * *

2   3-oz. pkgs. Philadelphia Brand cream cheese

3   tablespoons sugar

1   teaspoon lemon juice

½   teaspoon grated lemon rind

1   egg

Combine crumbs, sugar and margarine; press onto bottom and sides of 6-inch pie plate. Bake at 325°, 10 minutes.

Combine softened cream cheese, sugar, lemon juice and rind, mixing until well blended. Blend in egg. Pour into crust. Bake at 300°, 40 to 45 minutes or until set. Chill. Garnish with strawberries, if desired.

2 to 4 servings

Melon Magic

- 1 3-oz. pkg. Philadelphia Brand cream cheese
- 2 tablespoons milk
- 1 tablespoon sugar
- 1 teaspoon lemon juice
- 1 teaspoon poppy seeds
- ½ cup strawberry slices
- ½ cup green grapes
- 1 small banana, sliced
- ¼ cup shredded coconut
- 1 small cantaloupe, cut in half, seeded

Combine softened cream cheese, milk, sugar and lemon juice, mixing until well blended. Stir in poppy seeds. Spoon combined strawberries, grapes, banana and coconut into cantaloupe halves; top with cream cheese mixture.

2 servings

Dessert Crepes

- 3 eggs, beaten
- ⅓ cup flour
- ½ teaspoon salt
- 1 cup milk

      *   *   *

- 1 3-oz. pkg. Philadelphia Brand cream cheese
- 1 tablespoon sugar
- ½ teaspoon grated lemon rind
- ¼ cup Kraft red raspberry preserves

Combine eggs, flour, salt and milk; beat until smooth. Let stand 30 minutes. For each crepe, pour 1/4 cup batter into hot, lightly greased 8-inch skillet. Cook on one side only until underside is lightly browned.

Combine softened cream cheese, sugar and lemon rind, mixing until well blended. Spread four crepes with 2 tablespoons cream cheese mixture; roll up. For each serving, place 2 crepes on dessert plate; top with 2 tablespoons preserves.

2 servings

Note: Refrigerate or freeze remaining four crepes for future use.

SUBSTITUTIONS

For	Use
1 teaspoon baking powder	1/4 teaspoon baking soda plus 1/2 teaspoon cream of tartar
1 cup cake flour	1 cup minus 2 tablespoons all-purpose flour
1 oz. unsweetened chocolate	3 tablespoons cocoa plus 1 tablespoon fat
1 tablespoon cornstarch	2 tablespoons flour *or* 4 teaspoons quick-cooking tapioca
1 egg	2 egg yolks plus 1 tablespoon water *or* 2 egg yolks (for custard)
1 garlic clove	1/8 teaspoon garlic powder
1 tablespoon fresh herbs	1 teaspoon dried herbs
1 cup honey	1-1/4 cups sugar plus 1/4 cup liquid
1 cup fresh whole milk	1/2 cup evaporated milk plus 1/2 cup water *or* 1 cup reconstituted non-fat dry milk plus 2 teaspoons margarine
1 cup sour milk or buttermilk	1 tablespoon lemon juice or vinegar plus milk to make 1 cup (let stand 5 minutes)
1 lb. fresh mushrooms	6 ozs. canned mushrooms
1 teaspoon dry mustard	1 tablespoon prepared mustard
1/4 cup chopped fresh onion	1 tablespoon instant minced onion, dehydrated
1 cake compressed yeast	1 package or 2 teaspoons active dry yeast

EQUIVALENTS

Baking Items

Bread crumbs

Dry	1 cup	=	3 to 4 dried bread slices
Soft	1 cup	=	1-1/2 fresh bread slices
Flour, all-purpose	1 lb.	=	4 cups
Gelatin, unflavored	1 envelope	=	1 tablespoon
Graham cracker crumbs	1 cup	=	13 square graham crackers, finely crushed

Margarine

Regular	1 stick	=	8 tablespoons
		=	1/2 cup
		=	1/4 lb.
Soft	1 container	=	1 cup
		=	1/2 lb.
Marshmallows	1 regular marsh-mallow	=	10 miniature marshmallows
	100 to 110 miniature marsh-mallows	=	1 cup
Nuts, chopped (peanuts, pecans, walnuts)	4-1/2 ozs.	=	1 cup

Sugar

Brown	1 lb.	=	2-1/4 cups packed
Confectioners'	1 lb.	=	4-1/2 cups sifted
Granulated	1 lb.	=	2-1/4 cups

Cheeses

Natural chunk or process cheese	4 ozs.	=	1 cup shredded or cubed
Cottage	1 lb.	=	2 cups

Fruits and Vegetables

Apples	3 medium (1 lb.)	=	3 cups sliced
Coconut	3-1/2-oz. can shredded	=	1-1/3 cups
Lemon	1 medium	=	2 to 3 tablespoons juice
		=	1 tablespoon grated rind
Onion	1 medium	=	1/2 cup chopped
Orange	1 medium	=	1/3 to 1/2 cup juice
		=	1 to 2 tablespoons grated rind
Potatoes	3 medium (1 lb.)	=	2-1/4 cups cooked
		=	1-3/4 cups mashed

Rice and Pastas

Macaroni, uncooked	4 ozs. (1 cup)	=	2 cups cooked
Noodles, uncooked	4 ozs. (1-1/2 to 2 cups)	=	2 cups cooked
Rice			
Precooked	1 cup	=	2 cups cooked
Uncooked	1 cup	=	3 cups cooked
Spaghetti, uncooked	1 lb.	=	6-1/2 cups cooked

EQUIVALENT MEASURES

3	teaspoons	=	1 tablespoon
4	tablespoons	=	1/4 cup
5-1/3	tablespoons	=	1/3 cup
16	tablespoons	=	1 cup
2	cups	=	1 pint
4	quarts	=	1 gallon
8	ozs.	=	1 cup
16	ozs.	=	1 lb.
4	ozs.	=	1/4 lb.

INDEX

A

Ambrosia Pie, 140
Appetizer Paté Cheesecake, 14
Appetizers
  Cold (also see Dips and Spreads)
    Appetizer Paté Cheesecake, 14
    Blue Cheese Flan, 18
    Cheese Stuffed Celery, 24
    Ham 'n Pickle Pinwheels, 26
    Lunch Meat Stack-Ups, 27
    Party Egg Sandwich Loaves, 23
    Quick Wrap-Ups, 28
    Seafood Appetizer
      Cheesecake, 21
    Tasty Crabmeat Canapés, 25
    Zucchini 'n Cheese Stuffed
      Celery, 27
  Dips
    Clam Appetizer Dip, 21
    Hot Beef Dip, 19
    Hot Crabmeat Appetizer, 17
    "Philly" Guacamole Dip, 18
    Versatile Dip, 25
    Zesty Dip, 170
    Zucchini Chive Dip, 27
  Hot (also see Dips)
    Appetizing Tortillas, 170
    Curried Chicken Puffs, 20
    Nautical Appetizers, 17
    Sausage Rolls Canadien, 16
    Sensational Stuffed
      Mushrooms, 26
  Spreads
    Creamy Cheddar Spread, 24
    Cucumber Cheese Spread, 19
    Devilicious Ham Spread, 26
    Fruit 'n Cheese Spread, 23
    Impromptu Appetizer, 14
    Mock Paté, 15
    Nordic Style Tuna Paté, 28
    "Philly" Cheese Bell, 15
    Sherried Spread, 170
    Skyline Appetizer, 16
    Tropical Cheese Ball, 19
Appetizing Tortillas, 170
Apple Glacé Pie, 133
Apple Kuchen, 95

Apricot Cream Cheese Cookies, 143
Apricot Crumble Cake, 105
Asparagus Delmonico, 77
Avocado Cream Dressing, 55

B

Bagel Toppers, 37
Banana Raisin Bars, 143
Bavarian Apple Torte, 155
Bavarian Beef Sandwiches, 40
Beef 'n Corn Casserole, 85
Beefy Supper Treat, 82
Berry Cool Cheesecake, 127
Berry Patch Coffee Cake, 98
Berry Shortcakes, 178
Bewitching Blueberry Pie, 136
Blueberries 'n Cheese Coffee
  Cake, 97
Blueberry Cream Pie, 134
Blue Cheese Flan, 18
Brandied Cherry Coffee Cake, 94
Breads
  Apple Kuchen, 95
  Apricot Crumble Cake, 105
  Berry Patch Coffee Cake, 98
  Blueberries 'n Cheese Coffee
    Cake, 97
  Brandied Cherry Coffee Cake, 94
  Chocolate Ripple Coffee Cake, 98
  Crullers, 96
  Favorite Banana Bread, 99
  Glazed Sweet Rolls, 102
  Kolacky, 103
  Orange Nugget Coffee Cake, 106
  Orange Tea Ring, 104
  Philadelphia Nut Bread, 94
  "Philly" Brunch Cake, 101
  Poppy Seed Bread, 104
  Pull Apart Ring, 96
  Pumpkin Cheese Bread, 101
  Raisin Scones, 99
  Treasure Bran Muffins, 95
Broccoli Soup, 58

C

Cakes
  Bavarian Apple Torte, 155

Cakes
Berry Shortcakes, 178
Coconut Torte, 166
Holiday Gift Cake, 162
Individual Tortes, 180
"Philly" Marble Cake, 160
"Philly" Pound Cake, 153
California Burgers, 30
Carameled Pecan Pie, 138
Caramel Puff Pancake, 156
Carrot 'n Raisin Cheesecake, 110
Centennial Cheesecake, 109
Cheesecakes
Baked
    Carrot 'n Raisin
     Cheesecake, 110
    Centennial Cheesecake, 109
    Cocoa-Nut Meringue
     Cheesecake, 117
    Creamy Cocoa Cheesecake, 112
    Harvest Pumpkin
     Cheesecake, 111
    Hollywood Cheesecake, 114
    Lattice Cherry
     Cheesecake, 113
    Marble Cheesecake, 113
    Metropolitan Cheesecake, 115
    Orange-Butterscotch
     Cheesecake, 119
    Peanut Butter and Jelly
     Cheesecake, 118
    Praline Cheesecake, 118
    Strawberry Glacé
     Cheesecake, 122
    Sun-Sational Cheesecake, 120
    Supreme Cheesecake, 121
    Sweet Potato Cheesecake, 108
    Washington Cheesecake, 112
Refrigerated
    Berry Cool Cheesecake, 127
    Creamy Cool Cheesecake, 127
    Creamy Orange
     Cheesecake, 126
    Key Lime Cheesecake, 126
    Lemon Delight
     Cheesecake, 128
    Peppermint Cheesecake, 124
    Rocky Road Cheesecake, 123
    Special Occasion
     Cheesecake, 123
    Tom and Jerry Cheesecake, 108

Tropical Cheesecake, 121
Cheese Stuffed Celery, 24
Cheesy Beef Sandwiches, 36
Cheesy Tuna Snacks, 38
Cherry Cheese Chocolate Pie, 139
Cherry Cheese Delight, 157
Chicken à la Ring, 83
Chicken Corn Pies, 174
Chicken Divan, 174
Chicken Potato Bake, 91
Chicken Tacos, 30
Chiffon Dessert Sauce, 63
Chive Sauce, 64
Chocolate Angel Pudding, 168
Chocolate Chipper Bars, 144
Chocolate Cloud Pie, 132
Chocolate Cream Pie, 178
Chocolate-Orange Cookies, 142
Chocolate "Philly" Frosting, 155
Chocolate "Philly" Fudge, 152
Chocolate Ripple Coffee Cake, 98
Chocolate Soufflé, 158
Clam Appetizer Dip, 21
Cocoa Drops, 149
Cocoa-Nut Meringue
  Cheesecake, 117
Coconut "Philly" Fudge Balls, 163
Coconut Torte, 166
Coffee "Philly" Frosting, 160
Confections
Chocolate "Philly" Fudge, 152
Coconut "Philly" Fudge
  Balls, 163
Vanilla "Philly" Fudge, 157
Cookies
Apricot Cream Cheese
  Cookies, 143
Banana Raisin Bars, 143
Chocolate Chipper Bars, 144
Chocolate-Orange Cookies, 142
Cocoa Drops, 149
Cream Cheese Spritz, 149
Fudgy Nut Squares, 144
Lemon Glazed Jam Bars, 150
Lemon Nut Bars, 145
Marble Squares, 146
Nutty Coconut Drops, 146
Orange Almond Cookies, 145
Pecan Tassies, 142
"Philly" Chippers, 148
"Philly" Sugar Cookies, 149

Cookies
   Princess Brownies, 148
   Shortbread Cookies, 150
Corny Beef Bake, 84
Corny Cheese Soup, 59
Country Casserole, 88
Country Corn Casserole, 73
Cranberry Supreme, 154
Cream Cheese Kugel, 73
Cream Cheese Pastry, 132
Cream Cheese Spritz, 149
Creamy Blue Cheese Salad, 46
Creamy Cabbage, 74
Creamy Cheddar Spread, 24
Creamy Cocoa Cheesecake, 112
Creamy Cool Cheesecake, 127
Creamy Deviled Eggs, 38
Creamy Orange Cheesecake, 126
Creamy Orange Salad, 48
Creamy "Philly" Frosting, 165
Creamy Rice Dessert, 168
Creamy Turkey Tetrazzini, 89
Creme à la Maison, 161
Creme de Menthe Pie, 130
Creme Vichyssoise, 59
Crullers, 96
Crunchy Crust Peanut Pie, 137
Cucumber Cheese Spread, 19
Cucumber 'n Onion
  Sandwiches, 37
Cucumber 'n Onion Salad, 171
Curried Chicken Puffs, 20

D
Delmonico Sauce, 64
Dessert Crepes, 181
Desserts, Miscellaneous (also see
  Cakes, Cheesecakes,
  Confections, Cookies, Pies and
  Tarts)
   Bavarian Apple Torte, 155
   Berry Shortcakes, 178
   Caramel Puff Pancake, 156
   Cherry Cheese Delight, 157
   Chocolate Angel Pudding, 168
   Chocolate Soufflé, 158
   Cranberry Supreme, 154
   Creamy Rice Dessert, 168
   Creme à la Maison, 161
   Dessert Crepes, 181
   Fruit Dreams, 152

   Heavenly Cream Soufflé, 163
   Melon Magic, 181
   "Philly" Banana Pudding, 167
   "Philly" Fruit Pizza, 165
   Pineapple Cheesecake
    Dessert, 166
   Regal Banana Crepes, 167
   Seafoam Lime Dessert, 154
Devilicious Ham Spread, 26
Dill Sauce, 67
Double Cheese Soup, 60
Dressings
   Avocado Cream Dressing, 55
   Garlic Cheese Dressing, 55
   Ginger-Orange Fruit Dressing, 42
   Golden Fruit Dressing, 42
   "Philly" Parm Dressing, 56
   Poppy Seed Dressing, 56
   Roquefort Dressing Supreme, 43
   Sour Cream Fruit Dressing, 56

E
Emerald Isle Mold, 48
Empire Turkey Sandwich, 34
Epicurean Sauce, 67

F
Favorite Banana Bread, 99
Festive Chicken Salad, 51
Florentine Macaroni Bake, 92
Florentine Soup, 60
Frosted Pineapple Salad, 53
Frosted Sandwich Loaf, 35
Frostings
   Chocolate "Philly" Frosting, 155
   Coffee "Philly" Frosting, 160
   Creamy "Philly" Frosting, 165
   Vanilla "Philly" Frosting, 158
Frothy Lime Pear Mold, 49
Fruit Dreams, 152
Fruit 'n Cheese Spread, 23
Fruit Slaw, 54
Fudgy Nut Squares, 144

G
Garden Fresh Stroganoff, 81
Garden Macaroni Salad, 45
Garden Vegetable Spread, 39
Garlic Cheese Dressing, 55
German Chocolate Pie, 139
Ginger-Orange Fruit Dressing, 42

Glazed Sweet Rolls, 102
Gloucester Halibut, 90
Golden Fruit Dressing, 42

H
Ham and Cheese Bake, 89
Ham and Cheese Omelet, 176
Ham 'n Pickle Pinwheels, 26
Ham 'n Pineapple Casserole, 85
Harvest Pumpkin Cheesecake, 111
Hawaiian Spread, 40
Hearty Egg Salad, 52
Heavenly Cream Soufflé, 163
Heavenly Dessert Sauce, 69
Holiday Gift Cake, 162
Hollywood Cheesecake, 114
Honey Date Sauce, 69
Horseradish Sauce, 68
Hot Beef Dip, 19
Hot Crabmeat Appetizer, 17

I
Imperial Peach Salad, 49
Impromptu Appetizer, 14
Individual Tortes, 180
Italian Spaghetti, 91

J
Jubilee Sauce, 62

K
Key Lime Cheesecake, 126
Kolacky, 103

L
Lattice Cherry Cheesecake, 113
Lemon Cream Topping, 70
Lemon Delight Cheesecake, 128
Lemon Egg Soup, 61
Lemon Glazed Jam Bars, 150
Lemon Nut Bars, 145
Liver Sausage Snacks, 39
Long Loaf Sandwich, 31
Lunch Meat Stack-Ups, 27

M
Main Dishes
  Cheese and Eggs
    Florentine Macaroni Bake, 92
    Ham and Cheese Omelet, 176
    Italian Spaghetti, 91

    Mushroom Soufflés, 176
    Philadelphia Poached
     Eggs, 177
    "Philly" Brunch Quiche, 86
    Savory Scrambled Eggs, 81
    Spinach Mushroom Bake, 86
    Sunday Brunch, 80
    Vegetable Spaghetti, 175
  Fish
    Country Casserole, 88
    Gloucester Halibut, 90
    Tuna Broccoli Bake, 90
  Meat
    Beef 'n Corn Casserole, 85
    Beefy Supper Treat, 82
    Corny Beef Bake, 84
    Garden Fresh Stroganoff, 81
    Ham and Cheese Bake, 89
    Ham 'n Pineapple
     Casserole, 85
    Main Dish Popover, 80
    Meatball Stroganoff, 92
    Sicilian Supper, 88
    Simple Supper, 84
    Stuffed Manicotti, 177
    Supper Stroganoff, 175
    Winner's Spaghetti, 82
  Poultry
    Chicken à la Ring, 83
    Chicken Corn Pies, 174
    Chicken Divan, 175
    Chicken Potato Bake, 91
    Creamy Turkey Tetrazzini, 89
Main Dish Popover, 80
Majestic Spinach Salad, 51
Mandarin Fruit Pie, 140
Marble Cheesecake, 113
Marble Squares, 146
Meatball Stroganoff, 92
Melon Magic, 181
Merry Cranberry Freeze, 45
Metropolitan Cheesecake, 115
Mixed Vegetable Bake, 74
Mock Paté, 15
Molded Fruit Salad, 53
Molded Salmon Salad, 52
Mushroom Soufflés, 176

N
Nautical Appetizers, 17
Nordic Style Tuna Paté, 28

Nutty Coconut Drops, 146

O

Onion Cheese Soup, 62
Open-Face Denver Sandwiches, 33
Orange Almond Cookies, 145
Orange-Butterscotch
  Cheesecake, 119
Orange Cream Squares, 47
Orange Nugget Coffee Cake, 106
Orange Tea Ring, 104

P

Paradise Pumpkin Pie, 130
Parisian Wine Sauce, 66
Party Egg Sandwich Loaves, 23
Party Potato Bake, 77
Peanut Butter and Jelly
  Cheesecake, 118
Pecan Tassies, 142
Peppermint Cheesecake, 124
Perfection Vegetable Mold, 54
Philadelphia Hollandaise, 66
Philadelphia Nut Bread, 94
Philadelphia Poached Eggs, 177
"Philly" Banana Pudding, 167
"Philly" Brunch Cake, 101
"Philly" Brunch Quiche, 86
"Philly" Cheese Bell, 15
"Philly" Chippers, 148
"Philly" Chocolate Sauce, 64
"Philly" Club Sandwiches, 36
"Philly" Cranberry Pie, 133
"Philly" Fondue, 31
"Philly" Fruit Pizza, 165
"Philly" Guacamole Dip, 18
"Philly" Hard Sauce, 63
"Philly" Marble Cake, 160
"Philly" Parm Dressing, 56
"Philly" Pound Cake, 153
"Philly" Sloppy Joes, 32
"Philly" Sugar Cookies, 149
"Philly" Waldorf Salad, 43
Pies and Tarts
  Ambrosia Pie, 140
  Apple Glacé Pie, 133
  Bewitching Blueberry Pie, 136
  Blueberry Cream Pie, 134
  Carameled Pecan Pie, 138
  Cherry Cheese Chocolate
    Pie, 139

Chocolate Cloud Pie, 132
Chocolate Cream Pie, 178
Cream Cheese Pastry, 132
Creme de Menthe Pie, 130
Crunchy Crust Peanut Pie, 137
German Chocolate Pie, 139
Mandarin Fruit Pie, 140
Paradise Pumpkin Pie, 130
"Philly" Cranberry Pie, 133
Pineapple "Philly" Pie, 131
Regal Strawberry Pie, 131
Sunburst Peach Pie, 134
Sunny Banana Pie, 136
Sunrise Cherry Pie, 137
Tea Party Tarts, 153
Tropical Apricot Pie, 138
Twosome Cheese Pie, 180
Pineapple Cheesecake Dessert, 166
Pineapple "Philly" Pie, 131
Pink Sparkle Freeze, 42
Piquant Broccoli, 75
Pita Bread Sandwiches, 39
Poppy Seed Bread, 104
Poppy Seed Dressing, 56
Potato Chowder, 171
Potato Potage, 61
Potato Puff Extraordinaire, 76
Praline Cheesecake, 118
Princess Brownies, 148
Pumpkin Cheese Bread, 101
Pull Apart Ring, 96

Q

Quick Wrap-Ups, 28

R

Raisin Scones, 99
Regal Banana Crepes, 167
Regal Cheese Sauce, 66
Regal Rice Ring, 75
Regal Strawberry Pie, 131
Rocky Road Cheesecake, 123
Roquefort Dressing Supreme, 43

S

Salads
  Fruit (also see Gelatin)
    Fruit Slaw, 54
    Merry Cranberry Freeze, 45
    "Philly" Waldorf Salad, 43
    Pink Sparkle Freeze, 42

Salads
    Special Ambrosia, 171
    Sunny Fruit Salad, 43
  Gelatin
    Creamy Blue Cheese Salad, 46
    Creamy Orange Salad, 48
    Emerald Isle Mold, 48
    Frosted Pineapple Salad, 53
    Frothy Lime Pear Mold, 49
    Imperial Peach Salad, 49
    Molded Fruit Salad, 53
    Orange Cream Squares, 47
    Perfection Vegetable Mold, 54
    Zippy Zucchini Mold, 55
  Main Dish
    Festive Chicken Salad, 51
    Hearty Egg Salad, 52
    Majestic Spinach Salad, 51
    Molded Salmon Salad, 52
  Vegetable (also see Gelatin)
    Cucumber 'n Onion Salad, 171
    Garden Macaroni Salad, 45
    Unique Greek Salad, 46
    Zesty Potato Salad Ring, 47
Sandwiches
  Bavarian Beef Sandwiches, 40
  California Burgers, 30
  Cheesy Beef Sandwiches, 36
  Chicken Tacos, 30
  Cucumber 'n Onion
   Sandwiches, 37
  Empire Turkey Sandwich, 34
  Frosted Sandwich Loaf, 35
  Long Loaf Sandwich, 31
  Open-Face Denver
   Sandwiches, 33
  "Philly" Club Sandwiches, 36
  "Philly" Sloppy Joes, 32
  Pita Bread Sandwiches, 39
  Savoy Sandwich, 34
  Shrimpjohn Sandwiches, 33
  Sandwich Sauce Superb, 68
  Sandwich Spread, 37
  Sauce Louis, 63
Sauces
  Savory
    Chive Sauce, 64
    Delmonico Sauce, 64
    Dill Sauce, 67
    Epicurean Sauce, 67
    Horseradish Sauce, 68

    Parisian Wine Sauce, 66
    Philadelphia Hollandaise, 66
    Regal Cheese Sauce, 66
    Sandwich Sauce Superb, 68
    Sauce Louis, 63
    Sweet 'n Sour Sauce, 69
    Tangy Tartar Sauce, 68
  Sweet
    Chiffon Dessert Sauce, 63
    Heavenly Dessert Sauce, 69
    Honey Date Sauce, 69
    Jubilee Sauce, 62
    Lemon Cream Topping, 70
    "Philly" Chocolate Sauce, 64
    "Philly" Hard Sauce, 63
    Spicy Apple Sauce, 70
    Toasted Almond Sauce, 70
Saucy Broccoli, 172
Sausage Rolls Canadien, 16
Savory Mushroom Soup, 62
Savory Rice, 74
Savory Scrambled Eggs, 81
Savory Spinach Casserole, 73
Savoy Sandwich, 34
Seafoam Lime Dessert, 154
Seafood Appetizer Cheesecake, 21
Sensational Saucy Noodles, 78
Sensational Stuffed Mushrooms, 26
Sherried Spread, 170
Shortbread Cookies, 150
Shrimpjohn Sandwiches, 33
Sicilian Supper, 88
Side Dishes (also see Vegetables)
  Cream Cheese Kugel, 73
  Regal Rice Ring, 75
  Savory Rice, 74
  Sensational Saucy Noodles, 78
  Super Noodle Side Dish, 172
Simple Supper, 84
Skyline Appetizer, 16
Snacks
  Bagel Toppers, 37
  Cheesy Tuna Snacks, 38
  Creamy Deviled Eggs, 38
  Garden Vegetable Spread, 39
  Hawaiian Spread, 40
  Liver Sausage Snacks, 39
  "Philly" Fondue, 31
  Sandwich Spread, 37
  Snack Squares, 38
  Vegetable Pizza, 32

Snacks
Snack Squares, 38
Soups
  Broccoli Soup, 58
  Corny Cheese Soup, 59
  Creme Vichyssoise, 59
  Double Cheese Soup, 60
  Florentine Soup, 60
  Lemon Egg Soup, 61
  Onion Cheese Soup, 62
  Potato Chowder, 171
  Potato Potage, 61
  Savory Mushroom Soup, 62
  Vegetable Rice Soup, 172
  Zucchini Bisque, 58
Sour Cream Fruit Dressing, 56
Special Ambrosia, 171
Special Occasion Cheesecake, 123
Spicy Apple Sauce, 70
Spinach Mushroom Bake, 86
Spinach Treat, 78
Strawberry Glacé Cheesecake, 122
Stuffed Manicotti, 177
Stuffed Squash, 72
Stuffed Tomatoes, 173
Sunburst Peach Pie, 134
Sunday Brunch, 80
Sunny Banana Pie, 136
Sunny Fruit Salad, 43
Sunrise Cherry Pie, 137
Sun-Sational Cheesecake, 120
Super Noodle Side Dish, 172
Supper Stroganoff, 175
Supreme Cheesecake, 121
Sweet 'n Sour Sauce, 69
Sweet Potato Casserole, 76
Sweet Potato Cheesecake, 108

T

Tangy Tartar Sauce, 68
Tasty Crabmeat Canapés, 25
Tea Party Tarts, 153
Toasted Almond Sauce, 70
Tom and Jerry Cheesecake, 108
Treasure Bran Muffins, 95
Tropical Apricot Pie, 138

Tropical Cheese Ball, 19
Tropical Cheesecake, 121
Tuna Broccoli Bake, 90
Twice-Baked Potatoes, 173
Twosome Cheese Pie, 180

U
Unique Greek Salad, 46

V
Vanilla "Philly" Frosting, 158
Vanilla "Philly" Fudge, 157
Vegetable Pizza, 32
Vegetable Rice Soup, 172
Vegetables (also see Side Dishes)
  Asparagus Delmonico, 77
  Country Corn Casserole, 73
  Creamy Cabbage, 74
  Mixed Vegetable Bake, 74
  Party Potato Bake, 77
  Piquant Broccoli, 75
  Potato Puff Extraordinaire, 76
  Saucy Broccoli, 172
  Savory Spinach Casserole, 73
  Spinach Treat, 78
  Stuffed Squash, 72
  Stuffed Tomatoes, 173
  Sweet Potato Casserole, 76
  Twice-Baked Potatoes, 173
  Vegetable Stir-Fry, 72
Vegetable Spaghetti, 175
Vegetable Stir-Fry, 72
Versatile Dip, 25

W
Washington Cheesecake, 112
Winner's Spaghetti, 82

Z
Zesty Dip, 170
Zesty Potato Salad Ring, 47
Zippy Zucchini Mold, 55
Zucchini Bisque, 58
Zucchini Chive Dip, 27
Zucchini 'n Cheese Stuffed
  Celery, 27